KICKING

Derek Jarman – painter, theatre designer and film-maker
– held his first one man show at the Lisson Gallery in
1969. He designed sets and costumes for the theatre
(*Jazz Calendar* with Frederick Ashton and *Don Gio-
vanni* at the Coliseum). He was production designer for
Ken Russell's films *The Devils* and *Savage Messiah*,
during which time he worked on his own films in Super
8 before making his features: *Sebastiane* (1975), *Jubilee*
(1977) and *The Tempest* (1979). From 1980 he returned
to painting (a show at the ICA) and design (*The Rake's
Progress* with Ken Russell in Florence), and made the
films *Caravaggio* (1986), *The Last of England* (1987),
War Requiem (1988), *The Garden* (1990), *Edward II*
(1991), *Wittgenstein* (1992) and *Blue* (1993). His books
include: *Dancing Ledge* (1984), *The Last of England*
(1987; now republished by Vintage under the title the
author intended for it, *Kicking the Pricks*), *Modern
Nature* (1991), *At Your Own Risk* (1992) and *Chroma*
(1994). Derek Jarman died in February 1994.

BY DEREK JARMAN

Derek Jarman

KICKING THE PRICKS

VINTAGE

Published by Vintage 1996

2 4 6 8 10 9 7 5 3 1

First published in Great Britain
as *The Last of England* by Constable, 1987

Vintage
Random House, 20 Vauxhall Bridge Road, London SW1V 2SA

Random House Australia (Pty) Limited
20 Alfred Street, Milsons Point, Sydney
New South Wales 2061, Australia

Random House New Zealand Limited
18 Poland Road, Glenfield,
Auckland 10, New Zealand

Random House South Africa (Pty) Limited
PO Box 337, Bergvlei, South Africa

Random House UK Limited Reg. No. 954009

A CIP catalogue record for this book
is available from the British Library

ISBN 0 09 930227 6

Papers used by Random House UK Ltd are natural, recy-
clable products made from wood grown in sustainable
forests. The manufacturing processes conform to
the environmental regulations of the country of origin

Printed and bound in Great Britain by
BPC Consumer Books Ltd
A member of
The British Printing Company Ltd

PREFACE

This text was created in winter 1986 to spring 1987, during the editing and sound synching process for Derek's film *The Last of England*. Each day Derek would produce a handul of A4 pages illegibly handwritten in red Pentel: opinions; reminiscences; portraits of people and places; and audio-taped rambling interviews with friends and colleagues Derek had recorded that afternoon. Each night, as the production office wound down I would transcribe these tapes and writings; ending at midnight with a new sheaf of papers for Derek's corrections over chips and salt beef sandwiches in a nearby cafe. This was the height of Derek's fame from his association with The Smiths, and soon it became known when and where it was easy to meet him. On one night a superfan tracked him down, looked at both of us, and said accusingly: 'You're Derek Jarman', then turning to me – beef dangling from my mouth – said, with shock and some disappointment: 'And you're Morrissey?!!'

Derek extensively re-edited and re-ordered the text, scrubbing out the past, inverting meanings, ruthlessly cutting so that pages were returned bleeding from their red Pentel duels – a process of revision and re-invention that was characteristic in his painting, writing, film editing, and personal history.

Derek's original title was *Kicking the Pricks*, but in the name of synergy, and with some reluctance on his part, the volume came out as *The Last of England*, and faded into memory like the images in the film.

Of Derek's writings, I had always overlooked this volume, preferring the lyricism in *Modern Nature*; but on re-reading it before this edition went to press, found in it poetry, terseness, clarity and an anger that ameliorated with later years, all of which serve as a key to memories of a person and a time now misted.

Keith Collins, Prospect Cottage, 1996

ACKNOWLEDGEMENTS

I am grateful to the following for allowing me to use their photographs in this book: Mike Laye, Mark Plested, Isobel Schneyder, Ray Dean, Bridget Holm, Alastair Thain and the Anthony D'Offay Gallery. The photographs on the following pages were taken on location during the filming of *The Last of England* by Mike Laye and are copyright 1987: 38, 84, 87, 88, 91, 111, 162, 165, 168, 171, 174, 180, 192, 195, 201, 206, 209, 210, 214, 224, 228, 231 and 246. The pictures on pages 49, 61, 70 and 73 are by Ray Dean.

And thanks to Keith, Shaun, Nick, Mike and Stephen for all your help.

I

The Last of England started filming in August 1986.

These diary entries, interviews and notes for the script were written during the following weeks.

The book starts with my original ending for the film – The Ship Sails – and takes us on a journey back in time and forward into an uncertain future . . .

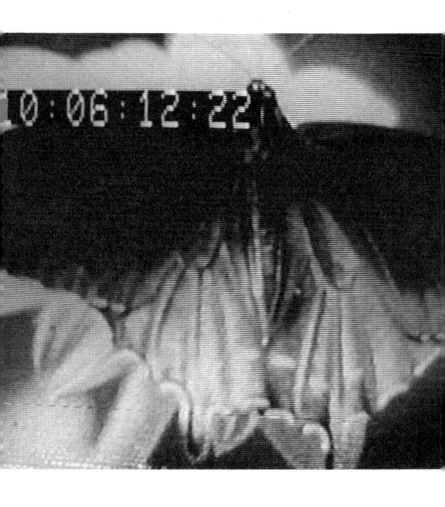

10 : 06 : 12 : 22

The Last of England: Psyche/Logos Soul/Word

THE SHIP SAILS

Elizabeth II's boarding Britannia. Flunkies with greasy ill-fitting wigs hold bunches of freeze-dried flowers, souvenirs of a thousand royal occasions. Lilibet brandishes her riding whip at the photographers.

'Fucking carrion crows.'

The words are drowned by the mournful siren of the departing ship. The cold March wind blows a patter of freezing hail. The siren wails. 'Hurry! Hurry! Hurry!' The Earl Marshal wheels on his charger, glowering under frosted eyebrows. Threadbare dukes and duchesses lugging mangy cabin trunks with fading stickers: Thomas Cook, P and O, Capetown, Sydney, Hong Kong and Singapore, struggle up the gang-plank. A jet screams overhead, Lilibet stumbles and her crown rolls into a thicket of barbed wire. A rocket flashes like lightning through the cold black clouds and explodes in the iron grey waves with a dull thud. A horse bolts and tramples a lady-in-waiting.

'Northumberland and Leicester, Dorset and Essex, all down Maam.' Lilibet, eyes blazing, whips the stragglers, kicks the unwilling corgis into the dock.

'Left, right, left, right,' barks the Earl Marshal. The ship sails over the horizon with its geriatric cast. Hell-bent for a rendezvous with their assets in Laguna, far in the jammy West where the Imperial sun has not yet set. Leaving the rotting shires to rot.

After they have gone, in the deathly silence a small boy dances on the quay, throwing a last stone for England and St George.

He returns home later.

'Where yer fucking been Johnny?'

'No one got killed in that film Mum. It's a con. Can't wait to grow up and get into *Star Wars*.'

EDITING THE LAST OF ENGLAND

The editing of *The Last of England* is going well. We clocked up 55 minutes of film this afternoon. Angus and I assemble the film as we go. Video editing, unlike film editing, is sequential, you go from A to B. It's very hard to hop around as each time you recopy the image you lose quality and eventually sync as the time code deteriorates. 55 minutes in two weeks is good going. We start at around ten in the morning and check out at about 5.30; six hours of watching the time code is exhausting and we start to slip like the edits in this simple machinery.

The machines also warm the room, so by tea-time it's suffocating. We edit about five minutes a day, the watershed was last Friday when we pieced together a disco sequence, cut like a pop promo. I brought it back home in the evening, and showed it to Shaun who up to this moment had been polite but rather indifferent; he lit up and said it gave the work an epic quality.

Music video is the only extension of the cinematic language in this decade, but it has been used for quick effect, and it's often showy and shallow.

The images in the disco are not arbitrary, although there is an element of chance in the way they rattle along. The cutting is staccato, and aggressive. It would not be possible

Imagining October: Angus Cook

to cut film this way, although theoretically you might attempt it. 1600 cuts in six minutes. The sequence crashes into the film unexpectedly, the pace is relentless. It should wind the audience. Why do I want to do this?

CHASING DRAGONS

Now every high street had a disco, people danced in the empty factories and warehouses. There was nothing for them to do, drink was abundant, the music grew louder and louder, it was better that way. Better the young should down cocktails than throw them, it was cheaper to invest in alcohol than jobs, it was an intelligent form of control. Johnny thought when all purpose had been forgotten the world would end this way, with a dance. He slumped back in a corner, drew his knees up to his chin, and watched.

Everyone had gone to bed hours ago.

The sensible ones.

As they slept, he'd passed through all the nine circles.

Now, the music was going to end.

The last song and dance.

Positively.

The last song and dance.

The lights came up, the cockroaches swarmed for cover in the cracks of the cancerous sweaty walls.

Stunned faces dissolved into the ashen dawn.

Johnny staggered to the gents. The last numbed boy moaned, as he was buggered by his mate in the cubicle,

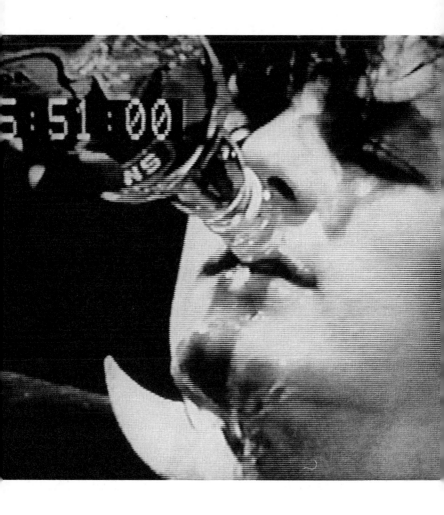

The Last of England: Disco

his dulled mind barely registering orgasm.

The boy turned, and looked at Johnny with bloodshot eyes.

'You wan' doin' too?' He spat onto the floor, dropped to his knees, and put Johnny's limp cock in his mouth. Johnny came as if fulfilling an obligation, evaporating like the last gaseous bead in the warm flat beer, he buttoned up. As he walked back home he passed the weary researcher, picking up *The Times* with his milk. 'What new diseases will he invent today?' thought Johnny.

On the empty dance floor the cleaners make rival plans for their summer holidays. Johnny picks up a discarded paper, 'Virgin Boss To Clean Up London'.

NOTHING TO BE AFRAID OF?
ARE THESE WORDS TOO BRAVE?

The young doctor who told me this morning I was a carrier of the AIDS virus was visibly distressed. I smiled and told her not to worry, I had never liked Christmas. I had put on my dark black overcoat I love so much to walk to the hospital. Wearing it at my father's funeral a few weeks ago I looked more sombre than the undertakers. It gave me confidence for this meeting. As I walked up the freezing street against the tide of Christmas shoppers I thought it was inconceivable I could have avoided the virus, though I had avoided the test for as long as was decently possible. Earlier this year the doctor had suggested

I took it; at the time I was coping with the furore that the showing of *Jubilee* on Channel 4 had stirred up, 4 am death threats on the phone. I felt insecure. I saw the news leaked to the *Sun* and the *Star* with visions of ending up as part of the daily diet of terror that sells these malevolent and jaundiced newspapers.

It was almost with relief that I listened to the doctor's catalogue of do's and don'ts—shaving, hairdressing, all the little details (soap and water it seemed eliminated the virus outside the body)—but for all of medicine you might as well just wash your mouth out with carbolic. The sword of Damocles had taken a sideways swipe, but I was still sitting in the chair.

Walking back down Tottenham Court Road from the hospital, I thought how fortunate to be forewarned so that one can wind one's life up in an orderly fashion. The finality of it seemed attractive.

As I joined the crowds at Oxford Street, I thought— could my perception of all this change, could I fall in love with it again as I did when I left home early in the 1960s?

The sun came out briefly, the thin wintry sun, so low in the sky it blinds you. The wind seemed colder than ever. I stopped at the stationers and bought a daybook for 1987 and a scarlet form to write out a will.

OLD EZ AND YOUNG P.P.

I'm reading about Ezra Pound in the ruins of his dream Italy, writing the Cantos caged in the Pisan prison camp at the end of World War II. I'm fascinated and repelled by him: mad, bad Ez and the usury business. Declared insane by doctors and politicians perjuring themselves to save the S.O.B. from the firing squad. 11 years in the St Elizabeth's asylum until back in Italy he gives the fascist salute as he docks at Naples; up yours!!

Meanwhile in Rome another poet and film maker, Pier Paolo Pasolini is being tried for armed robbery, the first of many trumped-up cases which will be brought by the Italian state. Old Ez fascist and young Pier Paolo communist share a common foe, the disease consumption: not TB, something more deadly.

For Ez it is the Roosevelt-Rothschild connection, a criminal banking system hell-bent on destroying value, with Benito his Saint George; but the dragon wins to consume Pier Paolo's Italy with its allies, the Christian democrats. Never trust a Christian. The Egyptians had scarabs, they have the death-watch beetle. These corrupters lay waste the mental and physical landscape of dear Italy in a sea of rubbish tipped all over the place, driving the autostrada del sol ever southward to its rendezvous with the Mafia, and Italy's most lucrative post-war industry: the heroin trade.

Old Ez and young P.P. allies: a nice conundrum to sleep on.

CHILD ABUSE

In 1945 my father was posted to Italy. Overnight home was transformed from the bleak wartime married quarters with their coke stoves and mildew to a villa on Lake Maggiore. Villa Zuassa had beautiful gardens. There I chased lizards among the enormous golden pumpkins that grew along the gravel paths, played hide-and-seek in alleys banked with camelias, or crept off to the gatehouse where a little old lady in the blackest mourning fed armies of silkworms on trays in the gloom of her front room. She would give me caterpillars and cocoons to take home, and I would be driven back through the woods by her grandson Davide on the handlebars of his bike. He would stop and hoist me on his shoulders to pick a particular flower. Davide was my first love and the love was returned. He rowed me on the lake as storms blew in from the mountains. This love was my great secret, if only this innocent idyll could have continued. But after a brief summer we left for Rome.

My first confrontation with oppression was in the cold dormitory of a British preparatory school a few years later, and the terrible battle with family virtue was on. My crime was prosecuted by the headmaster with more violence than any other misdemeanour in the school. I had crossed over the dormitory and climbed into the bed of another nine year old; the action was quite innocent, neither of us could have foreseen the consequences. An older boy reported us because of the noise we were making, laughing and giggling, to the headmaster's wife who descended on us like a thunderbolt from a clear blue sky. In a welter of oaths she tipped us out of the bed onto the floor. We were

My mother, my sister and myself

beaten, hauled up in front of the whole school, threatened with expulsion, and the terrible consequence our actions would have on our families if they were revealed. This public exposure gave me an incredible shock and opened wounds that will never heal. The violence of the attack drove my heart into the shadows, where it remained buried. I became detached and dreamy, spent hours alone painting or watching the flowers grow, had a physical aversion to chumminess and sexual innuendo, organised games, and school showers. I was set apart, a childhood observer who never joined in. The boys ragged each other: so-and-so's in love with so-and-so, and so-and-so is queer. From thirteen to eighteen I had no form of sexual expression at all. All my energy was devoted to painting while the other boys learned their four-letter vocabulary on the rugger pitch.

Do you think that odd? People would expect public schools to be a hive of sexual activity.

No. I've heard people had different experiences, but my school was puritanical, ran on muscular christianity punctuated by alarm bells. We lived in communal rooms, there was no privacy, we spent most of our spare time polishing our shoes.

How aware were you of your sexuality, it must have been in the background?

It couldn't be expressed, I just gave up. I wasn't attracted to any of the boys, if anything I was repelled by the all-male environment, the possibility of temptation made it worse. Many young men I talk to are aware of their sexuality from childhood; the attitude of their peers and their early encounters mark their development. There is no accepted pattern to growing up, you are at the mercy of chance. In my childhood there were no accessible patterns that were positive, everything was negative. It affected me deeply, I became a very backward kid, uncertain, terribly shy. I knew I was 'queer', and I knew that was totally unacceptable. None of my friends, either in school or in the austere world of the RAF stations were as far as I know in the same predicament. This would not change much at King's College, London.

After I left school in 1960, I had to commute up to the Strand each day from home. There was, however, one handsome young man who I used to see in the dining room; I used to hang around hoping we might get talking, but of course this never happened, and by 5.30 I was back on the Metropolitan Line.

One evening a business man exposed himself in the carriage—in my state this did more harm than good, and that summer, hitch-hiking back from Switzerland, I was picked up by a very unpleasant middle-aged man who drove right off the road and attempted to assault me. I was quite tough enough to resist, but he had locked my passport and money in the boot of his car, and threatened to turn me in to the police saying I had assaulted him. I was very frightened: after four hours of battle, he threw me out of the car as I was crying uncontrollably. It was hardly an auspicious beginning, but I don't think it was unusual.

In 1962 I moved to London from home. I was twenty, and out on my own. Things changed quickly. At King's I read my tutor's copy of *Howl*, and learnt of William Burroughs. The Drama Society put on *The Maids* and the first

British performance of *Blood Wedding* for which I did the sets.

It began to dawn on me that there were others, if only I could find them. The first person I confided in was a theological student from the college who was working in Bethnal Green. I walked from Bloomsbury to Bethnal Green and back each Sunday to see him, until one day I plucked up the courage to tell him. To my surprise he wasn't upset, just a little mystified. He said he had met some guys in New York, but none here. We didn't speak about it again.

A few months later I met an old school friend of mine who was living with his girlfriend and an older man, Michael. Michael seemed very eccentric to me: he would sit at his piano singing the songs he composed for unperformable musicals about buggery, and brewed homemade wine. I would sit on the sofa quietly, and every now and then he'd spin round on his piano stool and rag me. I would blush and he would pounce: 'Blushing, you're blushing.' But I never gave my secret away, though I was round there nearly every evening that year.

Just after my twenty-second birthday in 1964 a young Canadian lad Michael had met came round expecting to find him in. Ron asked if he could stay the night as it was late. There were no night buses, and my friends suggested I stay the night as well. As I was falling asleep Ron crossed over and got into my bed. I had reached the age of 22 without contact of any kind. It was explosive. Next day, when I woke, Ron had disappeared. I was unable to find him that evening, and in desperation downed a bottle of whisky without realising what I was doing. I poisoned myself so badly I spent the next two days in bed after a traumatic evening in which I slashed all my paintings in the flat and threatened to turn the scissors on myself. I was in tears for 24 hours before everything stabilised.

ALASDAIR

Alasdair is homeless again, staying at St Mungo's with the dossers. At first he refused to accept Christopher's invitation to stay for Christmas. He arrived here in the afternoon, but returned for a shower. At 11 we went out, after he had promised to move to Christopher's in the morning. Christopher had said, 'You're taking up a valuable bed at the worst time of the year, you have to move.' This did the trick.

Alasdair is now 35 and has never had a room of his own. He falls asleep on floors, or stays awake all night in the clubs. He retains all the sparkle he had years ago when he was a boxing blue at Oxford. I worry as he is not well.

We were in immense high spirits as we walked to Charing Cross. He remarked that I was crossing the roads with a reckless disregard for the traffic. 'Not like the old days when you crept about so cautiously.' I noticed immediately he told me. As the evening wore on a great calm descended. I'd crossed over and was untouchable. For the first time in months I was free from the tangle of fear that had grown up like poison ivy. Alasdair laughing and dancing through the night gave me courage. I left sensibly early to have a night's rest before our journey to Shropshire.

Alasdair McGaw

MIDNIGHT MASS

The bells that welcomed us to Ellesmere Church pealed out of tune; old and exhausted like the faithful, they seem to have lost their way. The midnight mass progressed like a VAT form with its sections and subsections written by many hands in some ecclesiastical tax office, watermarked HMSO, its purpose to dissuade the curious. Now, if you are like my friend Christopher, well ordered, you need a sense of mystery. Mystery is of course for those who cannot believe in their heart of hearts, 'Christ be with you'. Here in this church, coldly scrubbed by the Victorians, the new form of service is conducted at snail's pace, each section and subsection repeated and underlined by a gaggle of bri-nylon priests, who chase up and down their patch honking about the stable at Bethlehem. Four times we were invited to join in carols so impossibly high and halting — 'Hark the Herald', 'While Shepherds watched' — that only those deaf to their own voices can sing.

Christopher has frozen to the glumness of a gargoyle. I prod him into action; we're singing something about 'his wings', was he a fairy also?

Christopher grinds into a basso that vibrates the boys and girls playing at bad manners in the pew in front.

The door with its heavy Victorian latch crashes open with regular monotony. A punk girl with a purple face titters with her friend; shall I pass her a note saying 'I met Johnny Rotten' and shut her up? 'Oh come let us adore him'. The first two of the repeats of this carol have to be left to the 30 old ladies from The Grange Hotel; they're so impossibly high. At 12.30 on Christmas Eve this is the only show in town and the back pews are populated by

Christopher Hobbs

New York 1985

dissidents. A skinhead boy and his friends have arrived and sprawl across several side pews fingering the order of service with their love and hate tattoos. The Mayor, a frightened-looking bantam of a man with a skimpy silver chain, accompanied by a wife like a Christmas robin, looks apprehensive; perhaps the skinhead who is now rubbing his crotch through the sermon is his son.

The sermon is about the meaning of the stable. 'Let's go,' says Christopher. Everyone is now shaking hands and muttering 'Peace be with you'. The bri-nylon priests are advancing ominously up the aisle towards us in slow motion, stopping any hope of escape. Thank God I'm not at the end of the pew. Is this some ghastly left-over from one of those '60s theatre companies when you had to participate, or some TV show where an unsuspecting audience member is about to be dragged into the limelight to be made a fool of? A tall camp-looking boy, face pale as ivory under a black quiff, tight black trousers and white shirt sleeves, flounces off down the aisle to read inaudibly from Isaiah before returning with a broad grin which he wipes from his face with a limp wrist.

Down on your knees.

What are all these people doing? If heaven is conducted like this, half-threat half-chat-show, thank God I'm never going to get there. The girl in front has her itchy fingers twined round her boyfriend's crotch as we stand yet again. 'Christ be with you', he quickly adjusts himself as everyone suddenly turns and faces towards the back of the church. Now we can see the congregation staring past us with dull submission into the shadows. Thank God their God is a God of mercy. I don't mean to be unkind, but the priest is now preaching about their fears for the next year. If I came with some sadness or slight fear myself it has been dulled out of existence. Perhaps this is what the C of E is all about, a tedium that would send the living quite dead into the afterlife; and if, after all, heaven is like this, it should be no more difficult to cheat oneself in than fiddle the DHSS.

TIDINGS OF COMFORT AND JOY

I arrived two hours late for the edit this morning. A black panic swept through me during the night. It pounced on me, a tangible physical presence. I was jolted out of the first moments of sleep by a spasm which ravaged me like a bomb blast; after that I spent the rest of the night in a state of shock; all the emotion I had screwed down burst spewing phantoms which pranced in the dark.

The atmospheres that Christmas and New Year generate are so poisonous that I find them unbearable when I'm in the best of health. These long, bleak, empty days when the street below is charged with the mindless energy of the dispossessed, shouting, smashing bottles, blowing whistles and kicking empty beer cans. Punctuated by police, ambulance and fire sirens; stunned into silence momentarily by a delirious drunk weaving across the pavement bawling at his reflection in a shop window loaded with tinsel junk.

The few who have any business have long since disappeared to the suburbs; even the heroin addicts have faded away. Rubbish bags vomit the detritus of cheap parties

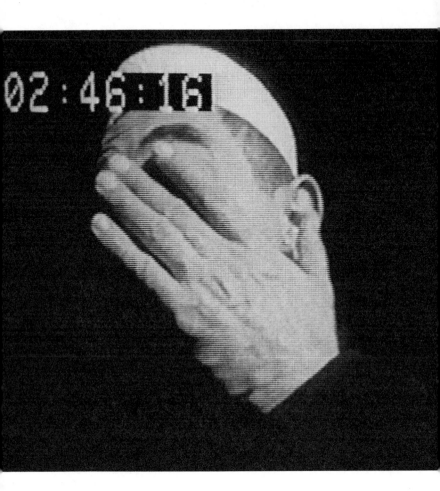

The Last of England

across the road. The unloved post is thrown into the hall below. Shops shut without warning; the bread, if you can find it is stale.

AMERIKA

1964. It was with relief I left for America in July to meet my new friend Ron. After 22 years in solitary, the door had opened a little, and a chink of light shone through. Like the prisoners in *Un Chant d'Amour*, we shared a cigarette.

I found out that the first student flight had been arranged to coincide with the end of the summer term, and I got myself a seat on it. Armed with a ninety-nine-days-for-ninety-nine dollars Greyhound ticket, I arrived in New York, knowing no one, but with the address of the priests that my theologian friend Roger had worked with in my pocket.

I had very little money. In those days you didn't have to declare your assets at the airport. I had one free night in the Knickerbocker Hotel, a midtown flea-pit where eight of us slept in a room. I was completely alone. The next day I walked the streets of Manhattan, very disoriented. I bought myself some cherry pie at an automat, struggled with the dimes and nickels, and rang up one of Roger's reverends who was working at the Episcopalian HQ around the corner from the United Nations. He told me to come around, leave my suitcase and tour the United

Nations building, the architectural 'hit' of the moment. I was dead keen on architecture: I had studied under Pevsner, at King's. 'Come back at 4.30 and I'll take you home,' he said.

We climbed into one of the yellow NY cabs, and we hadn't gone more than a hundred yards when he threw his arms around me right in front of the cab driver. We got to the Mission, where within minutes there was an open competition amongst the reverends to decide where and with whom I was going to sleep that night. These weren't your anaemic C of E reverends, they all wore tight jeans and sweat-shirts, one had tattoos and scars from a knife fight. They got me very drunk and late that night all piled into the bed and took turns trying to fuck me: nothing like this had happened before, this world I'd stumbled into seemed a mayhem. I kept my virginity. They put it down to English reserve and didn't hold it against me. The next morning was Sunday, so after breakfast we went to a church they called 'Mary on the Verge' which was used for cruising. The altar boys flirted with the congregation; I felt very uncomfortable. The next day I got the Greyhound to Calgary in Canada, to spend the summer with Ron.

In the afternoons we sat by the swimming pool where he had a holiday job as a lifeguard, and when his girlfriend turned her back, had it away in the locker rooms; or after everyone had left, in the pool. I got myself a job working on the City Survey. At weekends we drove to the Rockies and went swimming in the icy mountain rivers.

One afternoon we drove up to where the Canadian-Pacific Railway with its observation cars starts its long haul over the mountains. Even with two tenders the trains come past slowly, you could hear them coming as they sounded

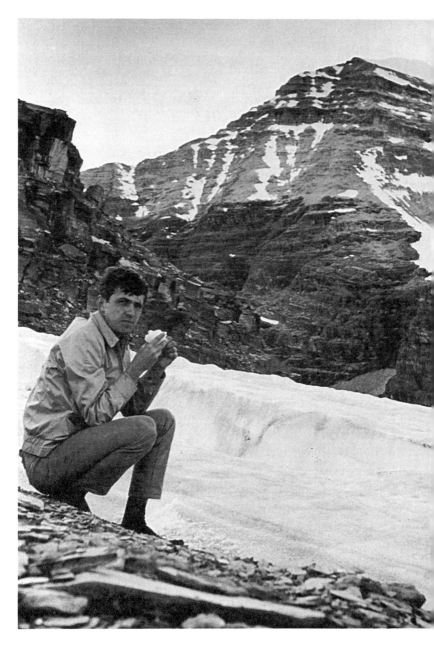

My photo of Ron 1964

Ron's photo of me 1964

their hooters. Ron decided we should sunbathe on the cutting, watching the trains pass.

After a couple went by he said, 'We should take all our clothes off.' We could hear another train coming. He threw his arms round me; as it went by, I could see the people in the observation cars staring at our wild embarrassed groupe. It was a moment of naked triumph, *We Two Boys Clinging Together.* As soon as the train passed we ran.

In late August I left Ron and took the Greyhound bus to San Francisco to visit the City Lights Bookshop. I'd crossed the world to get to that bookshop, to buy Burroughs's *The Naked Lunch*, banned in England. I bought my copy of it along with Ginsberg's *Howl*, and Kerouac's novels. I spent my days walking round San Fransisco and the nights reading. I didn't go to any clubs, I wasn't aware they existed; so far I'd met only Ron and the randy reverends.

In September I caught the Greyhound back to New York. On the way I had plenty of time to worry about which reverend I should sacrifice myself to. One seemed less obnoxious, so I rang him from the bus terminal, exhausted after three days and nights travelling across the States. He seemed pleased I'd called and invited me round. When I got to his place, he said: 'Dump the suitcases, we're going to a party.' I was so tired I was almost hallucinating when we arrived at an old run-down brownstone; room after room packed with black and white men, many of them in drag, swishing around the rooms saying, 'Who, who, who, is the most glamorous girl?' Unable to believe my eyes and ears, I retreated to a corner. After a time a young black man came up to me and started to chat; he grabbed me and took me into a bedroom. There he stripped me; I was game for this—I was so frightened by the others, he seemed my best hope of escape.

People kept coming into the room and throwing coats over us, one or two tried to get their hands on us, but he fended them off. He asked me where I was living; I told him the address, and he said, 'I'll take you back there.' I'd lost my reverend in the crowd so I couldn't tell him I was leaving. The two of us went back to the apartment, fucked in the hallway, and then fell asleep on the stairs. The reverend arrived at 6 am to find us locked in each other's arms on his doormat; he was furious; he threw my suitcase at me, and ordered us to clear off. It all seemed very passionate. We climbed into my friend's car and he drove me around New York for the rest of the day before putting me on the 'plane to London.

My parents met me at Heathrow. I must have looked a complete wreck, because my mother said, 'What have you been up to Derek?' I hadn't slept properly for nearly a week.

Life was slowly returning to the suburban routine, when to my absolute horror, I started to itch. I found what looked like a black scab and when I scratched it, it crawled. I didn't know what it was, so I told my mother I had been invaded by some awful insects. She laughed and said she didn't know what they were, I'd better go and see the doctor.

Our family doctor eyed me with suspicion, took out an enormous book, one of a series of serious-looking tomes, and flicked the pages, slowly and deliberately as if to prolong the agony. Finally he said, 'The cure is really dangerous, it's mercury. Have you been sleeping with prostitutes, Derek?'

I was tongue-tied, it hadn't occurred to me these monsters were transmitted by fucking. I looked at him and the words froze in my mouth; then in desperation I blurted: 'Yes.'

The Last of England: Richard Heslop, Chris Hughes and Cerith Wynn Evans

EMPTY SPACES

My first films filled in the empty spaces of my painting, then I lost heart with the painting. But I've come back to it; it still isn't a full-time occupation; but if I become ill it will be a way of working, quick, and gentle. I often think of Matisse, bedridden, cutting out 'Jazz'. If necessary you can work in bed. I see painting as a lifeline. I've worked frenetically since last August, I've never worked so hard in my life: *The Last of England*, pop promos, this book, and the paintings; I've been abroad—to America twice, Germany, Italy. I was painting during the filming of *The Last of England*, I painted eight paintings on New Year's day. The new paintings are very direct. The crucial moment is smashing the glass, I must be the only painter who shuts his eyes, as he completes his work.

Do you shut your eyes as a film-maker?

Do I shut my eyes as a film-maker? I'm impatient, I'm impatient with the paintings, it annoyed me they took so long, it still does, even though they take ten minutes. There's a moment when you know a painting's not working; you either destroy it, or you push it over the edge, and make it a complete mess; then leave it as a failure. It's not something I would do with a film.

What, if anything, do you discover while painting?

I don't think that any one painting brings discovery, it happens in the process.

I meant in the process.

The process is a struggle, the product always annoys me, it's unnecessary. It's all about process, I want people to notice the process, so that is why I keep my paintings. I could never quite understand the '60s painters who wanted their paintings to fall to pieces, it wasn't as if the 500 years they could have lasted was very long. Everything falls to the ground like dead leaves, making a rich compost, Greek statues are pulverised for lime, Roman wall paintings decay and fertilise, others grow out of them. Imaging is pre-conscious. I was painting at the age of four; before I could talk. My painting was as coherent as my conversation. I was painting seriously. My mother drew the patterns of her clothes. Nada Zaganovitch, a Yugoslav refugee living with my parents in Rome, painted the ruins. I still have her painting of Salita del Grillo; I went out with her every afternon to the Forum.

The first thing I painted at my preparatory school was a table mat with the school crest; I found it in my father's house after his death and threw it away. Already by eight I was well advanced: everyone agreed that I was going to be a painter, painting gave you the keys to a charmed life. At the age of 13 I read the 'romantic' lives: Van Gogh, Monet, Gaugin. I was academically backward, I found it difficult to express myself in words, there was always a sense of inferiority which I feel even now, a feeling my work didn't measure up; I could never believe anyone liked it. This was complicated by the '60s, the glitzy social world I entered. I wrote in *Dancing Ledge* that I was influenced by my times in ways that I didn't imagine.

You strike me as having been quite a serious adolescent?

40

I was serious, but in order to swim I had to throw away my lifeline to the past. It was the '60s, IT WAS GETTING BETTER ALL THE TIME. Did I survive it? I don't know. Did any of my generation survive it? Does it matter? If I'd turned my back I would have got nowhere.

'By turning your back on it you would have got nowhere.' How stifling was the '60s bourgeois bohemia?

It wasn't bourgeois bohemia, that was much older; it was the bohemia of the new media, of the TV, the coffee table book, the colour supplement. In this country it prided itself on being classless.

How did you fit in?

I was painting landscapes, close to the red earth of north Somerset, the flowers, butterflies in the meadows. My influences? William Scott's pots and pans, Paul Nash and the megaliths. It was impossible to paint these landscapes at the Slade in 1964; everyone was falling over themselves for pop-art, we were focussed on Manhattan. The 'new' art was an urban art, the art of the glass-topped coffee table with the flower arrangement on it, the comic, the poster: one measured oneself against that.

There were other 'strands': the large coloured abstracts, Morris Louis, Richard Smith. I loved Ron Kitaj's work, but his serious concern was invaded. There were gnomes everywhere in the '60s, suburban gnomes like Peter Blake.

I couldn't stomach the jokiness of the '60s, that complicity with rubbish, but I found that I myself was more than adept at this rubbish game. I played it with Ken Russell, who saw himself as a pop artist. Of course, he wasn't; Ken was the Music Hall, the vulgar joke, the drag artist, the pantomime, life in black and white, a cut out.

It wasn't all like that. There were elements in all of us that eschewed the rubbish. When I saw David Hockney's Cavafy etchings of very ordinary young men in bed together, they were something quite new; if you look at Cocteau's boys, they were idealised; these were very honest. David was honest to the point of naïvety. In the middle of all this I was very unsure of my direction, so unsure that I never painted in the Slade. I painted at home.

Your sexuality determined the kind of friends you made?

Yes.

Did you regret that?

It's impossible to answer, do I regret? If I hoped to find orgies, they weren't orgiastic; if I hoped to find permanence, it wasn't permanent. Deep down it was unsatisfactory, neurotic, but this was forgotten in the excitement.

What about careerism? This must have been very evident amongst your friends?

I ran from it. I was embarrassed by it. I hated the idea my paintings would end up above that coffee table. After all, it was the world I was trying to escape from.

What about your painter friends, like Keith Milow?

Keith changed. He was ruthless when he was younger, he knew exactly where he wanted to be. He was very serious about that.

What happened to your serious nature? Where did it go?

It was occluded by the brightness of this new world; after a life in an English public school and suburb, I think that's understandable. Whether it nourished me is another matter.

Why didn't you go to New York?

Oh I didn't go because I was frightened, frightened of losing . . .

Do you think that was OK?

No.

And what about your friends who went?

I think they were cast adrift, the Americans never embraced them. Perhaps they were lost before they went.

What were they after in New York?

Sex.

What else?

Money.
Power.
They saw it as a possibility, the possibility of . . .

What do you think about the art world then?

Well, art was already monitored by the CIA; that started in the McCarthy period in the '50s. (This still goes on—I'm on the computer at MI5.) The most expensive living artist was to become Jasper Johns who painted the Stars and Stripes. Art was tied to the apron strings of the very rich, and the auction houses.

You imply that by that time modern art had lost its audience.

No, a new class was enfranchised.

It's a very complicated situation. The people who bought art in the 20th century were *nouveau riche*, hardly ever old money. The newly rich merchants bought Picasso and Matisse in Russia; nothing changed, but what has changed is that those who bought communicated their good taste and satisfaction to the world through the colour supplements; the whole world knew they had bought a Warhol; in the old days they talked about it amongst themselves. Now they were able to sell their values to a much larger audience. This happened in the '60s.

BAD BOYS

What was it like to be young in the early '60s?

I was a nice middle-class boy, I didn't go drinking in Soho,

In 1960 I looked quite innocent

I was home by seven to swot up my Anglo Saxon for the next day's tutorial. The bars were an illegal world, far away from Metroland. All my spare time was spent painting. I was quite happy, perhaps I gave you the wrong impression—I didn't give sex a second thought. I listened to the monks of Solemnes, not Cliff Richard! I spent my holidays touring the French cathedrals. It was only after I discovered sex that it became a problem, perhaps I'm making too much of it.

At 21 I could have made a good monk and had no problem being celibate. Quite a few of my friends thought I would take orders. If you look at this photo I'm an innocent, happy as a sandboy. My life was ordered. The golden boy at King's who entranced me in the lobby was forgotten: out of sight, out of mind. He looked great on crutches tho' when he broke his leg in some accident, but I looked at him quite innocently, with admiration. I was looking at his blue eyes not the bulge in his blue jeans. One afternoon he appeared in the lobby, sweaty from a game of squash, and took his T-shirt off to wipe his face. I thought he looked beautiful.

After I returned from America I discovered a new world. I met David Hockney, Patrick Procktor, and Ossie Clarke, all of them at the beginning of glittering '60s careers. That winter David danced with us at the Slade dance: it is difficult now to imagine the effect this had, it was like diving for the first time from a very great height. David was a 'star', not just a good painter, but—like Warhol—at the cutting edge of a new lifestyle which was the most enduring legacy of the '60s. We would enjoy ourselves, something the repressed hated. Our openness hurt them. This sense of fun wasn't just hedonism, though it might have degenerated into that by the end of the decade.

Being open had more effect than one thousand committees. We had seized the initiative, so when the law was changed in '67, it seemed that the Great Debate was another generation coming to terms with itself. During the next four years I found a world which cut across barriers. We were economically advantaged. There was immense generosity, Patrick Procktor was very generous. At 23, the five years' difference between us made him a grown-up. There were a lot of private parties; if you were young and bright the doors opened. The gang who ran the Royal Court theatre were particularly lively. The straights fought back with words like 'decadent', a euphemism for queer.

Decadence, I soon learnt, was the first sign of intelligence. It's important to put the dance in an historical perspective, visual statements like David's golden hair—he said 'Blondes have more fun'—gave all of us hope, opened new horizons; now everyone's got a hairstyle, it's no longer operative.

We spent the rest of the decade celebrating wider horizons, throwing out the furniture, sitting on the floor, in brighter and brighter clothes. The music grew wilder, the Beatles were displaced by The Who and The Stones, they in turn by The Doors and, unlike today, we danced to the hits and often sang them aloud on the dance floor:'369 / The goose drank wine / The monkey chewed tobacco on the street car line.'

The last person to do this was Ossie, much later, who sang with irony in The Sombrero Club in London, 'I'm so vain, I think this song's all about me', at the top of his voice. But that was much later, a lot happened between.

This summer I played Patrick Procktor in Steven Frears's Joe Orton film. Steven's designer had reproduced

Patrick's studio in Manchester Street rather accurately. Pat must have been in his late twenties when he drew Joe, I felt a bit like mutton dressed as lamb, I was now 44. It was a very strange sensation.

'How do you want me? Bollock naked?' said Gary Oldman, standing in front of Pat's 'Long Live The Great Leap Forward' that I had watched being painted all those years ago. For the film I had a gorgeous paisley shirt but at the time I was wearing a roll-neck sweater, jeans, and donkey jacket. I appear in the foreground of the complementary picture 'Shades' wearing these. Patrick wore quite simple shirts, green trousers, and sometimes a little eye-shadow. We all put on slap for an occasion: for the Slade dance out came the kohl, panstick, and henna—I glued a very realistic plastic fly onto my face, as if it were crawling into my mouth.

It gave old ladies on buses quite a turn.

CINÉ LIFE

What was life like then?

Night life?

Yes.

I started to go out in the winter of 1964. The bars were small, the biggest was Le Duce in D'Arblay Street, with

Anthony Harwood and Ossie Clarke

a juke box in the corner. Clubs like this were not licensed, though there were drinking clubs like The Colony, and The Arts and Battledress. There were coffee bars like the Stock Pot in Panton Street, which was above ground, open to the street and a bit furtive. La Douce was the most fun. That's where the Mods went. It had a coffee bar upstairs, and a small basement for dancing downstairs. The boys who went there took purple hearts. Have you tried to dance thro' the night on weak Nescafé?

La Douce was open very late at the weekends, the sun was up before it closed its doors. I used to walk back home, there were no night buses. If you had nowhere to sleep off the night you probably ended up at a fleapit in Victoria called The Biograph. The Biograph was famous. It was run by the brother of the boxer Henry Cooper, with a geriatric staff, cost about 3/6d (probably less), and was always half-empty, except on Sunday afternoons when it was so packed you had to stand in the side aisles.

It was quite a large cinema, its programming as eccentric as its clientele. It showed German health and efficiency films set in Bavarian forests, naked girls prancing around with large steins of beer, and gents with short leather pants. But the next day they might have Pasolini's *Porcile*.

A few OAPs and tramps slept in the back rows, while the lads played musical chairs. You weren't allowed to change chairs just like that; if you did, one of the staff would loom up with a torch like a monster from a vampire film—they showed quite a few of those. You had to make it official by a trip to the gents, which was right in front of the screen.

Every now and again the police showed 'interest'. On those days the staff were put on red alert, the place looked like the height of the blitz, torches like searchlights everywhere. If someone was caught with his hands in someone else's flies they were thrown out, hastily buttoning up, illuminated up the aisle, sometimes into the arms of a young police constable. It was real fun, every now and then someone would bump into an old tramp, perhaps molest one by mistake, and all hell would break loose. The tramp would get up and start shouting 'Fuck you'. People would shout back 'Fuck off', the torches would be flashing everywhere. It was perfect for a rainy afternoon, and made a trip to the cinema very exciting. You never knew what you were going to see, or whom you might meet.

CLOSED CIRCLES

Most people are lonely, and live in closed surroundings (misery of town dwellers—from Babylon to Sodom and back). Closeted people in the street have little knowledge of other worlds. They might have heard of them vaguely, read about them in their colour supplements, but they don't enter. The most they can do is have a circle of their own.

There are family conspiracies, youth conspiracies, political parties, professional conspiracies—circles in circles: churches, covens, lodges, chambers of commerce, mafia, MI5.

Enterprise allowance? Don't be lonely and paranoid: give your life a purpose and join a conspiracy!

OUR TIME

Andy Warhol's world of transvestites, transexuals and very sexy boys seemed like the best thing in the world. It was also much more open and immediate than anything here in London. We agreed he was the most important artist of our time, he mirrored America to perfection, if he had a fault it was his accuracy. However much I wanted all of this, I knew I couldn't fit in; I hadn't lost my passion for the Gregorian chant, so I kept my distance, I felt a slight drawing back.

My degree at King's had polarised my work into words and images. I had designed stage settings there, for the first British production of Lorca's *Blood Wedding*. At the Slade I worked in the theatre department, on designs for Proko-fiev's *Prodigal Son*, and Stravinsky's *Orpheus*, which drew heavily on Rauschenberg's Dante drawings. My paintings were quite different and more formally constructed. A painting called 'Landscape with Devices' won the Stuyvesant prize at the Young Contemporaries in 1967, but I was part of a second generation. The new generation had established themselves, and David Hockney was paint-ing 'Home': our homes. The path seemed blocked, I didn't want to be a follower.

Sex crept into my work through the theatre, particu-larly in the underworld scenes in *Orpheus*, for which I col-laged several American Physique Pictorials, splicing them with Richard Avedon's pictures of mental patients.

One lunchtime Bill Coldstream, the Slade professor, came into the theatre department, and gave me a bleak lecture, squinting at my designs of naked men in chains. But he didn't attack them directly, he talked of his role

My father filming 1953

as a film censor, and his dislike of psychological violence in *Whatever Happened to Baby Jane?* As I was fairly uninterested in the cinema at the time, it was strangely perceptive.

Meanwhile my paintings, unlike my theatre work, became emptier and emptier; their titles tell the story: 'Stony Ground', 'Cool Waters'. My final picture of the decade was called 'Deserts'. Then I picked up a Super 8 camera in 1970 and started to populate these dreary pictures with my friends—clothed, I should add; I was too shy to get their pants off on camera. These Super 8 films record the life of Bankside and Butler's Wharf. They are home movies, an extension of my father's and grandfather's work. The difference, of course, is that they don't record family life.

How do these short films relate to the more obvious stand you took in Sebastiane?

The home movie is bedrock, it records the landscape of leisure: the beach, the garden, the swimming pool. In all home movies is a longing for paradise. How have the victims prepared themselves for their brief immortality? Who smiles when they are told? Whose hair is brushed? Where is the serpent lurking? My grandfather's film tells you more about the 1920s than many a film constructed in the studios. Then everyone walked arm-in-arm, kids have a strangely formal manner, there are nannies to comb their hair, Imperial Airways flies them to Calcutta.

This home-movie making continued into *Sebastiane*.

I never saw myself as a film director, I've never seen myself as one, I'm not one.

It was impossible to foresee the outcome when we went

to Sardinia. One thing that did change was that now I was public property, and, unlike David Hockney, didn't have the protection of the fine art world. I was as bollock naked as the boys in the film.

INFERNO

When my last riverside warehouse burnt down in 1980 I sat through the night, entranced by my burning past.

The climb up through the dark and empty building to my studio at Bankside gave you a sense of foreboding. The greatest fun was bringing some unsuspecting boy back late at night, unpadlocking the old wooden doors of the derelict building, walking him through the cavernous spaces barely lit by dusty lightbulbs—until I opened my door on the top floor to reveal 'The Studio'.

It seemed that the sun would never set on our charmed life there, even rainy days dissolve in the memory, sprawled out of a summer's evening on the cushions made from old Dutch carpets found in the flea markets of Amsterdam. We lay high over the Thames in the arched windows that came down to the floor; the light from the river reflected in sinuous patterns on the beams, the phosphorescent stars on the glasshouse glimmered. 'Daphnis and Cloé' on the hi-fi.

At moments like this the room transformed and glowed upon the waters. I lay in the hammock in a peacock tie-dyed shirt, little gold swallows studded across my jeans, bright yellow boots, hair growing even longer, more and more audacious earrings: a metal fly, a scarab beetle, a coral and pearl drop.

The boys arrived in radical dresses. On acid the room

Bankside 1970, the greenhouse bedroom

was dew-dropped with light and still as a Vermeer. Like the incoming tide, the music lapped against the rafters till dawn crept up: purples, scarlets, oranges, and blues between the black Doric columns of Cannon Street railway bridge, a temple submerged in the Thames.

One by one the early trains sparkled over the river, bringing the city to life: and as they did so the lights in the skyscrapers went out, the cleaners went home. Below, in the river, the tugs with magical names like 'Gypsy' and 'Elegance', so low in the water they might sink, chugged past, their high chimneys belching dark smoke, towing strings of barges that dwarfed them; stacked with yesterday's rubbish in a swirl of screaming gulls. I threw open the windows and the gulls swooped for the crusts of bread held at arm's length.

Alasdair woke up. Half-dressed, he put on a hat, and I took a photo, out of focus. We walked along the river to the site of my first studio in Upper Ground, now demolished, and he took a photograph of me sitting on the doorstep, which was all that was left. Then we walked over Hungerford bridge to Charing Cross, from where I took the train to Northwood to have Sunday lunch with my parents.

That evening at six we all met up at the National Film Theatre to watch Fellini's *Clowns*, and afterwards, fifteen of us wandered back along the river, circus music still ringing in our ears—that insistent, serpentine music with its sinister jollity.

Back at the studio we sat, watched the sunset, and drank Vouvray. How laughable, the ugly conversions, the extortionate prices for the rich dimwits who came late. I had it all, like the full moon that came up that night, for nothing.

Alasdair out of focus. Easter day Bankside 1970

Alasdair's photo of me 1970, outside the front door of upper ground

DEAD TO THE WORLD

Part of my interest in the magician John Dee was his pre-occupation with secrets and ciphers.

Why this obsession with the language of closed structures, the ritual of the closet and the sanctuary? the prison cells of Genet's *Un Chant d'Amour*, the desert encampment of Sebastiane; Anger, insulating himself with magick, screening himself off; Cocteau's *Orphée*, an attempt to steal through the screen into the labyrinth and usurp the privileges only the cabal of the dead may confer; the wall of unreality that girds the house in *Salò* and its victims, who are told: What is about to take place here will have never happened, you are already dead to the world outside.

PSYCHO DEALER

That night started on the star-shaped, glass dance floor of The Sombrero in Kensington; afterwards we dropped acid in the cab. The bars of the late '60s and early '70s were no longer as closeted. The Continental Baths in New York, the most exciting club of the lot, were host to the social register on Fridays. The Baths were on the West side above Columbus Circle, in an old building: eleven dollars entry. The dance floor was alongside a very large swimming pool with fountains, surrounded by beach chairs. Off to the side was a labyrinthine white-tiled

1970 at Bankside

Turkish bath whose corridors ended in pitch black. The scalding steam took your breath away; in the darkest recesses a continuous orgy was under way, but the heat was so searing that only the most intrepid could get it up.

Besides the Turkish bath, there were saunas, a hundred bedrooms, a restaurant, a bar, a games room, and a hairdresser's, backrooms with bunks, pitch-black orgy rooms and a sunroof; on a weekend it would be packed. It was possible to live there and at 11 dollars a night cheaper than an hotel, or apartment. I met one young man who had lived there for three months; he had only left the building a couple of times.

Like the desert, though, the Baths played disturbing tricks, down there where time dissolved you in the shadows. The handsomest were the drug dealers, sprawled out on their bunks, gently masturbating, their doors slightly ajar to trap the unwary, and if you swallowed their bait, inhibitions cast aside, you'd be making love in that swimming pool, packed with naked bodies. Later, in an apartment crawling with cockroaches, staring at the ravaged features of some Adonis whose caked make-up had cracked like mud at the bottom of a dried-up lake, not all the fountains could restore the dream. This life could become as wearying as the treadmill in a rodent's cage; round and round we went in the land of Cockaigne.

DREAMTIME

How did your reactions to America change?

The longest period I spent in Manhattan was the four months of Summer 1974. I had a very wild summer. I wanted to work, but without a green card it was quite impossible. I would walk around Manhattan aimlessly during the days and went out on the town every night. By the end of that summer I was living at night. I was on the verge of being trapped in this American dream of liberated sex. Out every night on the piers, or at the Continental Baths; out at Fire Island, sleeping rough and meeting people on the beach. This night-life was charged with an excitement far greater than drugs; as you stepped into the dark you entered the world of strangers, on the derelict piers you left the imprisoned daylight world behind. The ground was strewn with glittering glass from the smashed windows, every shadow was a potential danger, you kept your money in your shoes. You walked through a succession of huge empty rooms, with young men often naked in the shafts of light which fell through the windows. The piers had their own beauty; surrounded by water, they were a secret island.

Out at Fire Island the atmosphere was the same. The shrubs in the woods that lie along the shore were heavily scented, full of fireflies, silent floating will-o'-the-wisps. The silence and deep satisfaction of being alone and accountable to no one attracted me as much as the possibility of a chance encounter. I would spend every night wandering, then sit by the sea-shore watching the sun rising. This world had a purity that one never encounters

The Last of England: Amerika

in 'civilised' surroundings. Living this way could preserve a cherished anonymity. As the decade wore on, I grew further and further away from the social events, the cocktail parties and openings, even my own studio. Out alone at night one was a traveller. Power, privilege, even good looks, certainly money, disappeared in that dark.

As long as this sexuality was contained underground, it could be exploited; the authorities never forgot to let you know it was to be contained. A bookshop or a poem could bring down the whole silly weight of authority. The works of the nineteenth-century abbess Hildegard of Bingen were seized by customs. The Churches decided that as long as relationships were not consummated they could be tolerated; a chief constable in direct communication with God could talk of our life in the cesspit.

The lid was off, the dance was on, and then suddenly the dance was over. Sex and drugs, though, mixed from the beginning. There's no one I know who hadn't experimented; it was hard to imagine inquiring intelligence without the mix. The nineteenth century was on opiates, everyone had drug experience then—Dr Collis Brown's Tincture, which my grandmother dosed us with, was:

Liquid extract of Opium / 10% Morphine.
1.4% Chloroform.
5.73% Proof Spirit.
Extract of Capsicum.
Oil of Peppermint.
Glycerine.

You bought it over the counter.

In the bars of the mid '60s it was purple hearts, hash;

acid rang in psychedelia. Back in 1960 I got hold of *The Doors of Perception*, Huxley experimenting with hallucinogenics. The Huxley book should definitely be read by all film students; it contains more useful information than any film textbook I've read.

COUGHING IT UP

I'm interested in work that has no obvious function, or should I say compunction? Perhaps out of this could come the most interesting work of all. I gave a lecture about this last night, would I be freed to make something more gentle? I've always felt driven: I burned to make *The Last of England*, I feel I have to write this book, coughing and spitting with bloody bronchitis, but after this? I feel no necessity to make another film—that interests me. I said to the audience 'Why am I here? What can you possibly learn?' I have taken all the steps to be co-opted by pulp, my films have made me a personality. The only way to restore order is *silence*, I always wanted to entitle a film *Silence is Golden*; you can just see the reviews: 'Why didn't he shut up?' The world is a cacophany of voices, the airwaves are jammed. Mayday. In this mayhem it is impossible to communicate anything serious any longer.

Is it a new economy of working? Is there anything to tell any longer?

The Tempest: 'Stormy Weather'

That's something I have to work out when we start filming this September; where did the refugees from *The Last Of England* go? Should there be great calm, after the stormy weather? I think of the film taking place after *The Tempest*. Did Miranda's marriage solve the world's problems?

The interesting thing about Dancing Ledge *was the kind of status which you gave to the word 'creativity' which I think was a symptom of pressure, to get around the extremely frustrating* Caravaggio *project.*

Looking back, those years were not wasted, they were years of distillation; I was in the retort, screwed down, I drew in my horns. I was out every night, there was nothing to do during the daytime, the nights came out of extreme frustration. I exploded on street corners, I hardly recognised myself. Everything seemed set against me, the political climate—even the weather.

You were under-employed? So you cruised.

There was nothing else to do. Every path now ran into closed doors, it was difficult to keep a sense of purpose. I carried the script in a briefcase with my friend Padeluun's sticker 'Diese Maschine Ist Mein Antihumanistiches Kunstwerk': his job was restocking the condom machines on the autobahns, he had them printed and slapped them on.

During which periods of your life did you have a sense of purpose?

I certainly had a sense of purpose when I was a teenager, I knew exactly what I wanted to do. I painted seriously as a 16-year-old, as seriously as a kid of that age could do, right to the moment I went to the Slade. At the Slade I was working in public, I found that very difficult, I found it easier to fuck in public! (But of course that's not true.) I think it would be better to say that during much of the sixties my life was divided, I had so many conflicting strands to bring together, film did that later, it re-established purpose in my life.

You began to lose your sense of purpose when you hit the scene?

Oh yes!

Also a particular sophisticated strand?

Yes.

. . . in which you were completely overshadowed by people like Hockney, did you feel stunted?

I felt nervous, I was very self-involved, the success of my friends weighed me down. That's why the relationships were often uncomfortable. I found that success stunted, it seemed parochial. The only person at the time who perceived this was Anthony Harwood, who said, 'You are better than all of this.'

He kept telling me like a missionary: 'You should not be paying attention to David Hockney or Patrick Procktor. You have far more resources, Derek; they are pygmies.' He kept saying, 'They are pygmies.'

It was flattering, I wanted to believe him, but at the same time didn't have the courage to believe in myself. He treated me seriously, he had seen his life destroyed by

Anthony Harwood

socialites, more international and more extraordinary than the socialites of our scene; we were queens but he knew princesses, real ones.

He was acutely sensitive, he realised he was trapped, that he was never going to do *it*, whatever *it* was; he didn't have the structure, he had sold *in*. He saw me as someone who might fulfil the promise, it wasn't an easy relationship, he was very critical. He saw the world I had collided with was necessary, but—there was a big but—but then he'd say 'You must experience these situations, in order to grow through them,' so he took me out to dinner with the Rothschilds. I didn't say anything about this in *Dancing Ledge* because I didn't have the courage to . . . sound self-inflated.

I don't think that is self-inflated really because it is someone else's advice and it is like . . .

He set about showing me things and informing me, he introduced me to books that he was interested in: *The Tale of Genji*, which he loved. I was given Ouspenski, from that came Jung. He was the person who put me in touch with soul. Anthony was a witch, he had a strong intuitive drive, he lived by intuition, this frightened other people, it made him suspect.

When you call somebody by name you have a power over them.

Mastery.

That's what witches are supposed to be particularly good at, and it's only children and schizophrenics who really appreciate that. It's common in mental illness to fear that if someone has your name they have an extraordinary, almost life-and-death power over you.

So I was diverted, it was a long diversion, now I'm more in tune with myself. I admired myself more at 18: quiet, introspective, and very self-contained.

Do you think there is any connection between that and the fact that you first had sex not at 18 but in your early twenties?

Yes, that changed me. I had no wish to be one of the fathers. Nevertheless I'm not certain that I discovered my sexuality—having struck out so strongly—it's not that I'm about to turn straight, but I regret the cutting off that the exploration of this sexuality caused. I regret my perspective. I never wanted to be strident, rather I wanted to be in tune, to sing songs.

You talk about isolation as a younger person; were you relieved to discover your group?

Yes, I was really happy to meet Patrick and David, they were great. When I was 18 I was so very much alone, I was working things out quite successfully alone in my painting, but . . .

And it was really all upset by a randy Canadian?

Not just a randy Canadian. It was like this: when you are fourteen, you become aware that there are other artists; before puberty you work unconsciously, you are not aware of the others. At the moment you become aware that there is a pursuit called painting, that's all right, you

At the Slade, 1966

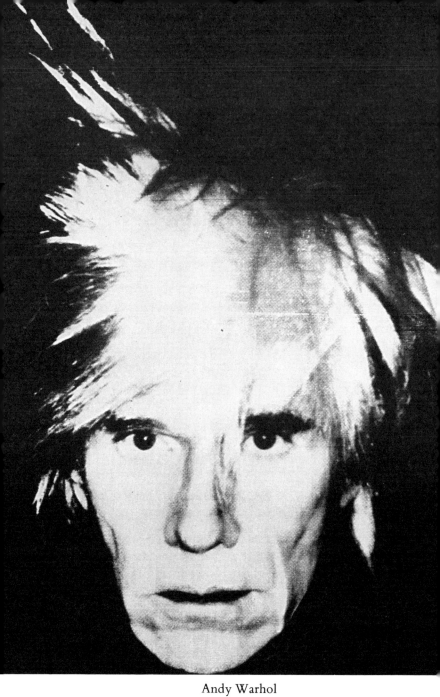

Andy Warhol

could overcome that. I would paint like Van Gogh, I would copy, I didn't feel embarrassed about copying. It didn't strike me that copying was a bad thing. The next thing I learnt was that I had to become an individual, individuate, to become myself; you can only do this alone; I was doing this quietly and quite well even at eighteen.

Then I went to The Slade, where I joined up with millions of the fuckers who were being taught to become themselves; I joined the crowd, it was crowded being an individual.

ANDY WARHOL IS DEAD

Warhol's death,
Let's mention Warhol's death,
WARHOL IS DEAD,
That's important that—WARHOL'S DEAD.
Did Andy Warhol die the moment Valerie Solanas shot him?
Did Andy Warhol die in '68?
Has he been inhabiting a department store since?
Well . . .
The wigs changed and slipped.
The thing about the wig is that the more it looked like a wig, the less it looked like a wig. Was it a wig? Because the wigs that look like wigs are the ones that attempt to look like real hair, and Andy's hair never looked quite like a wig.

There's something frightening in those last self-portraits,
  like God's flashbulb had gone off in his cadaverous face,
Death haunted Andy and the people round him, like
  moths in God's flashbulb.
It's the core of his painting.
He is a truly dead mirror,
Jackie Kennedy, the electric chair, Marilyn Monroe, the
  car crash, Elvis Presley, Brillo pads—how dead are
  Brillo pads?
The symbol of . . . the scourer,
THE DREAD SCOURER,
Yes they're a symbol of death,
Horrible frothy pink things rather like the colour on the
  paintings, sorry silk-screens, silk, silk-screen, silk is
  important to Andy, not cotton or linen, silk.
I see Andy Warhol as a plague image, leading the dance
  of death,
Circling round in the sulphurous smoke of society, Andy
  the black death, at a wake in the castle, a contrived
  wake,
Self-conscious, a million-dollar wake. One of the last
  paintings he painted was the Last Supper, a dying
  picture restored into destruction; he got into that party
  as well?
No.
He was at the edge of the party, they queued to get the
  AW on the edge of their A to Bs later.
When did he appear?
Where did he appear?
Why did he appear?
1964 was the year I first heard of him, he was a headline,
  he remained a headline till he died.
The most important artist of his time, no doubt about it.

The Times obituary ended 'he was a slight man who wore
    a blonde wig'.
It was impossible to mourn Andy,
I couldn't mourn Andy,
It was just . . .
He'd gone, like the '60s,
He'd gone, I didn't feel any sadness at all, he didn't die,
    he slowly EVAPORATED, he dissolved.
Saying 'Gee great'
'Oh I liked that, that was nice.' He always said 'yes' to
    everyone
'Gee great!',
'Yes!', 'Yes!',
'Gee great!'
It didn't matter he had died, after all he was only famous
    for 15 minutes, and he was, as I've said already, in the
    department store; he mirrored the culture that was
    dying with him.
What culture?
American culture!
You know, shoes, Brillo pads, soup cans, car crashes,
    Jackie, Marilyn, and Elvis,
It was, they said 'a great loss'.
Great?
Yes!
Great!

STEP FORWARD INTO THE PAS
THAT IS NOT

INTO THE MERRIE OLDE LAN
OF
WAS

Imagining October

II

IN WHICH WE MAKE A BLIND DATE WITH CONSUMPTION

Young bigots flaunting an excess of ignorance. *Little England*. Criminal behaviour in the police force. *Little England*. Jingoism at Westminster. *Little England*. Small town folk gutted by ring roads. *Little England*. Distressed housing estates cosmeticised in historicism. *Little England*. The greedy destruction of the countryside. *Little England*.

As I watched the documentary on the death of Pier Paolo Pasolini last week, I thought: what would he have made of *Little England* in the '80s? Pier Paolo's enemies saw him as a radical, but in fact he fought for traditional values, he even wrote against the students of '68 throwing stones at the police. Why didn't these students, the fortunate ones, throw stones at the real source of repression: the bankers and judges, rather than these simple boys from the south co-opted by the state?

Pasolini got his targets right. I wonder if he would like my films; like his, they are made in an older tradition, and this is why they are misunderstood by TV execs from the fleshy world of advertising, co-opted by consumption. The unions are also in complicity with this market, and would rather work for a $£\frac{1}{4}$ million perfume advert, than a serious feature film made for the same amount of money. There is no defence of value in these valueless circles. If Tarkovsky had had the misfortune to be born in Great Britain I doubt if he would have been able to make a single film; in the Soviet Union he worked with difficulty, but he worked.

Looking at my film-making from 1980 to 1987, I find

I have received £550,000 from all sources, with this I've established a reputation as a film-maker world-wide. The current going rate for one low-budget feature is three times this—about £1½ million. As I look for a further £200,000 for *The Last Of England*, thoughts bubble up: why is a film-maker like myself not funded? Is it my sexuality? When I made *Sebastiane* in 1975 I was open about it. Just how has this affected things?

Back to PPP, Laura Betti said the problem was his sexuality. He was always prejudged. Moravia said that in the end there was no conspiracy about his death. The climate was created so the boot boys could go in and murder him, feeling proud of it. What does this tell us? In our less extreme culture (or is it any longer?) we do things differently, don't we? It's been evident to me from the handling of my films that the problem was that I was queer, which precluded me for overt collaboration. A straight programmer would find no emotional entrées into the relationships in *Caravaggio*. Whereas someone in an audience could come out crying.

This year the billboards proclaim 'Would you like your children to grow up young, gay, and proud?' I presume the answer wasn't 'Yes'. It's going to be a cold hard decade for some of us, we will be treated as the virus in the body politic. One MP has already called for 'concentration camps'. These sinister times are very different from those far-off days when Enoch Powell's rivers-of-blood speech was so vilified. I think for those of us who have crossed over we should take heart in being positive.

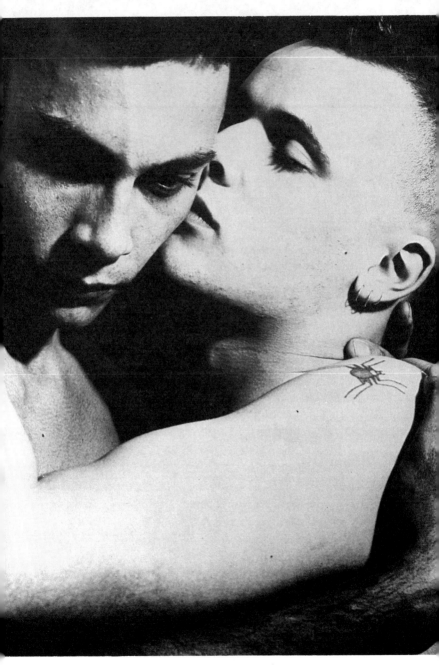

Angelic Conversation

Caravaggio: Nigel Terry

THE TEDIOUS TALE OF CHANNEL 4

NOW EVERY WELL-PAID JOKER WAS IN ON THE ACT.
OR, HOW A WELL-INTENTIONED ORGANISATION, DEDICATED
TO HELPING AN IDEA,
CAN END UP DESTROYING IT.

The Tempest opened in the Spring of 1980 with good reviews. I was congratulated by friends, 'Wonderful, Derek, you won't stop working!' But all of us forgot the power of capital, and the narrowing it creates. A culture geared to 'teeny-bop' and instant return is not too interested in ideas. In this world the survival of an artist is a fashion or a fad. The money required to make a film, let alone a consistent cinematic career, can evaporate like snow in June. There is always someone else to fill the little magazines. I found this out gradually and painfully during the next five years until *Caravaggio* was finally made.

The early 1980s were the dismal era of the British Film Renaissance, which helped no one. The invention of a new TV channel, which announced it was to make low-budget features, seemed like a ray of hope. But who would make their cinema? The Channel opened its doors in 1983, now would they make films with independent film-makers of the '70s? With Terrence Davies, with Sally Potter, Bill Douglas, Ron Peck or Julian Temple? Who else had made independent films? I had made three, which was the record of the DIY school. These film-makers had made excellent films: *Gold Diggers*, *Nighthawks*, *The Trilogy*. There were others, 'further out'—like Peter Wollen, would they be included? Sadly, the greening we expected never happened, there would be no green pastures for us.

The Channel quickly and efficiently put barbed wire across our prairie. The 'Wild West' was tamed. Now, when one went to producers for finance they said: 'We would love to make your film, Derek, with Channel Four.' Great! If the Channel wanted to make a film with you, but the TV men were less than enthusiastic; they were here to sell advertising and our films didn't complement the ads.

My first three films were bought early in the decade, with many others, for transmission (£12,000 for *The Tempest*, much less for the two others. Behind the cordial façade the sharks cavorted) and I had a new project, *Caravaggio*, in front of the panel. Translating the life of a painter onto the screen would be difficult, but with my background, it seemed to me I could perhaps make a go of it.

In the months before they opened Channel 4 overspent their budget and had to jettison a few projects. The experience of dealing with them in those early months was byzantine. Nicholas Ward Jackson, the producer, never quite knew who we should talk to; each time he rang there was a new voice on the line. I put it down to teething problems, but it became obvious by June that the wool was being pulled over our eyes, something was going on which no one was prepared to admit. A smoke screen had been put up, and three features were ruthlessly dispatched. Amongst them *Caravaggio*, and *Flight to Paris*. Chris Petit flew to Germany to solve his problems; he knew investors there. I didn't have those connections, I was stuck here.

I went up to the Edinburgh Television Conference in September, and let fly. It was an impossible situation as nothing of course could be proved. I was termed an 'hysteric', or later by one executive, a 'fascist'. I left Edin-

Caravaggio: Tilda Swinton 1985

Caravaggio: Sean Bean

burgh, exhausted, penniless and disillusioned.

Eighteen months after the opening of the Channel, my films were shown one morning at a preview theatre—the Bijou—so the new champions of the British cinema could find out what they were dealing with. On New Year's Eve *The Star* devoted the whole of its front page to 'The films which should never be shown to your kids': *Nighthawks* and *Sebastiane*. Within a week, a spokesperson, Paul Bonner, wrote to the *Telegraph* (of all newspapers) to say that the Channel had no intention of showing *Sebastiane* in the forseeable future; it had been bought as part of a package. The *Telegraph* wrote a humorous leader.

At that point I realised I had a real battle on my hands if I was to survive. Every now and then I would hear that Channel Four 'would like to show the films', but enquiries got nowhere. I was told they were waiting for an acceptable moment to put them out. Would it be in my lifetime? Could I make a film in this country? Caravaggio's life had all the elements of sex and violence that fouled up *Sebastiane* and *Jubilee*.

In 1985 David Robinson, the film critic of *The Times*, was given an opportunity to put together a season of films. He chose my three films, to be shown in reverse order. *The Tempest*, was to come first, to soften up the audience, then *Jubilee*, thought to be less offensive, and the horrible *Sebastiane* last, with David warning the audience. Of British independent feature-makers I had the honour to be the last to have my work shown. The Channel's monopoly had stopped me in my tracks for five years.

None of the programmers could understand they were the obstacle, and if they did, they appealed to some deluded fair play; you know the sort of thing: you're not the only film-maker, everyone should have a chance—it sounded egalitarian, but in reality they doled out the cash to their chums, and well-established film-makers from abroad.

The showing of the films was greeted by a roar of disapproval. During the early months of 1986 the Video Nasties Bill revolved around them. Jeremy Isaacs defended them on two 'Right to Reply' programmes. When Michael Winner said at BAFTA I was making pornography, Jeremy, with a wry smile, said I was a genius. That made me chuckle. Back at the House, MPs were shown violent excerpts from *Jubilee*. The Video Nasties Bill went down in May, as *Caravaggio*, which had finally been commissioned by the BFI (ironically with money from Channel 4, which had effectively privatised this institution) opened. I NEVER WANTED, OR MADE MY FILMS FOR, THIS TELEVISION AUDIENCE, OR THEIR BLOODY CHILDREN. But they bought them, they put them out, and they created this situation; if they had never existed I could have carried on working quite easily.

To keep myself occupied during those years, I took up my Super 8 camera, deciding to develop a parallel cinema based on the home movie which would free me. A space where I could paint my garden. I started *The Angelic Conversation* and *Imagining October*.

The Nizo Super 8 camera

IMAGINING OCTOBER

SHOT IN THE SOVIET UNION AND GB
16MM COLOUR, 27 MINUTES
MUSIC GENESIS P. ORRIDGE AND DAVE BALL.
PAINTING BY JOHN WATKISS.

In September 1984 Peter Sainsbury, head of production at The British Film Institute, invited me to Moscow to show *The Tempest* with other low-budget features. The trip was planned for ten days early in October. I had to make a short film for a late-night screening at the London Film Festival in November. I decided to film during the visit. I packed ten cassettes of Super 8 in a zap-proof lead bag and my Nizo 480.

As we came down through the clouds over Moscow it looked as if we were landing in Copenhagen, or any other Northern European city.

I expected the airport to be full of armed guards, like Paris or Rome, but apart from a few young soldiers there were none. We weren't searched at the airport, only a cursory glance, our luggage was X-rayed but nothing unpacked. My lead-lined package was ignored.

We were met by our guide, Bella Epstein, who took charge of us on the journey. In her early seventies, she reminded me of my grandmother.

We drove into Moscow as the sun was setting; the road was lined with the same drab suburbs of any major city, there was no advertising except for the occasional mural in the Soviet style—of muscle-bound figures frozen in revolutionary conformity.

Our hotel, the 'Peking', was all candyfloss columns and

Imagining October: The Hotel Peking Moscow

pastel turrets. Inside, the first thing I noticed was the anarchy of Russian interior decoration. The red carpet in the lobby, instead of going from the door to the stairs, took a sideways swipe in the direction of the coat check, and hit a blank wall. Where the hand of the state stops there's precious little symmetry.

Light switches are never aligned, as if drunken workmen had thrown darts to decide their placement; wires zig-zag across rooms in the most peculiar way, to lights which also bear no observable relation to the rooms they are lighting; it's a subtle art form! Three telephone kiosks next to each other, one leans like the tower of Pisa. Even the flower arrangements are asymmetric. My room was big and comfortable and had a large painting of chrysanthemums high up in the corner. There was a plug in the bath.

We stayed there during our visit, attending seminars, showing our films, and watching recent Soviet films in Dom Kino, the Union building. In the evenings we walked through the city, went to the state circus, and the Bolshoi.

The Soviet films were a surprise. There were films that paralleled 'commercial' films in the West. Films in this category could have two hundred prints made of them, and be shown to an audience of millions. Then there were films for more specialist audiences, and other films which, as here, might fall through the net entirely. Among the many fine films we were shown Alexei Gherman's *Twenty Days Without War*, and a quite extraordinary student film from Leningrad, with photography and sound-track very like David Lynch's *Eraserhead*. This film had a dazzling sequence; set deep in the winter, at the height of the seige of Leningrad, an orchestra, wrapped, against the cold like tramps, trudge through the snow past huge ships frozen in the Neva. One of the old men walks through the rooms of a ruined palace, its floors deep in snow. Snow even covers the ornate furniture, snow is falling in the rooms. He stops by an old wardrobe and scrapes the frost off the mirrors, and digs the snow to open a low drawer, from which he pulls out an old dinner jacket to dress for the concert. At the end of the film we see a newspaper photograph of the orchestra from the '40s, which fades to the real thing: the man who has dressed in the dinner jacket is the horn player, the music Tchaikovsky, the lady announcer says, 'This is Leningrad calling London.'

After several days in Moscow we flew to Baku, an old sea port on the Caspian at the centre of the oilfields. As we drove into town Peter Wollen, who had been here ten years before, said 'We have an erroneous perception of the Soviet Union; from the West we only look as far as Moscow and forget what lies beyond.'

If you compare Soviet Azerbaijan with the other part of this country in Iran, it has the appearance of a modern, well-organised society; with health care and education, it is noticeably well-ordered. Cross the border and you go back to poverty, disease and a feudal society.

In the old centre of Baku there was none of the destruction commercial development has caused in Western cities. The town was full of surprises—a mosque had been restored and turned into an apothecary's shop, selling herbal medicines, the packets beautifully designed, with names in Latin and Cyrillic. Baku had the leisurely air of an Edwardian resort; it had a promenade with palm trees and hibiscus, where everyone walked in the evening. There were floodlit pool tables under trees, with young men still playing late at night, and old men selling old fashioned lemonade at a penny a time.

The head of the film studios who met us from the plane (each of the Soviet republics has its own film industry) said, 'I am certain that you are pleased to get away from Moscow, you'll find it's much nicer down here, we have the sun and it's a bit more civilised.'

When we got to the Institute he said, 'I know you are down here to work, but surely you would like to have some tea, and time to see our city.' Austerity went out of the window, as tea was served with delicious meringues.

That evening we were invited to the theatre, where we saw a play set in the middle ages about rival Azerbaijan and Georgian families. It was easy to understand, performed as it was in song and dance.

After it was over we walked back to our hotel through the town; on the way we passed the monument to the Thirteen Commissars whom the British hung when they invaded the south with the White Army. The monument was a gilded 'Soviet brooch' with an eternal flame. I said to our host, 'This must be the monument to the Thirteen Commissars.' 'Yes, it's horrible kitsch isn't it? Tomorrow we'll show you some real sculpture,' he replied.

The next day we were taken to a Zoroastrian fire-temple, with a perpetual flame fed by an oil seepage. The temple had been turned into an ugly museum, with tableaux vivants of Zoroastrian monks torturing each other in the cells. The courtyard was deserted, it was raining, I filmed the flame and used it in *Imagining October*. Afterwards, we drove through an industrial wasteland, to a little house. Behind its walls was a garden of vegetables and flowers, where an old stonemason had built a folly: an extraordinary construction of concrete and tiles with sculptures of deer, dolphin, and mermaids around a great ramp spiralling like the remains of a shell. At the top was a room lit by peacock windows of stained glass, draped in fabrics and carpets.

The old man told us it had taken twenty-five years to build this memorial to his daughter, who had drowned in the Caspian sea. I told him it would be impossible to build like this in our country—you'd never get planning permission, it would be pulled down by the local council as a dangerous structure.

Back in Moscow; my *Tempest* and Sally Potter's *Gold Diggers* had caused tension with the officials. Soviet question and answer sessions are democractic, all questions go through the chair, the exchange of information is directed. This procedure is an iron lung.

Our afternoon session opened formally, there were cordial speeches. But when they stopped, a lemon-faced critic got up and said he had seen Zeffirelli's *Romeo and Juliet*, which he described as 'meretricious and vulgar'; 'but', he added, 'at least it had a point, unlike Derek Jarman's *Tempest*'. The audience strained forward for my reply, but before I could say anything, the chair intervened to add in English, 'Dare I—or may I coin a phrase—Derek Jarman's "camp" *Tempest*' and added something derogatory about Sally's feminism. 'Well, I wish I had brought my film *Sebastiane*, sexual pluralism and feminism are important issues . . .' I replied.

Bella translated this word for word, I felt the audience move uncomfortably; from that moment Sally and I became non-persons, neither *Gold Diggers* nor *The Tempest* were taken to Baku, and questions were subtly deflected.

On my last day we visited the small flat that housed Eisenstein's English language library. Many of the books were brought at Zwemmer's in the Charing Cross Road,

Imagining October: Eisenstein's copy of
Ten Days That Shook The World

they still had the receipts in them. The library was extensive: Dickens, Chesterton, Joyce, Wyndham Lewis, many of the books had dedications; both Joyce and Freud had given him their work. On the wall was a Mickey Mouse cartoon from Walt, and a signed photo of Charlie Chaplin.

Among the books Peter Wollen discovered a copy of Reed's *Ten Days That Shook The World*, signed 'Eisenstein, Moscow 1920'. It had been crudely censored: Trotsky's name blocked out in black ink; on this Eisenstein had based the official film of the Revolution *October*.

I had been filming the flat, with the consent of Mr Kleeman, the curator; I filmed Peter turning the pages of this book, nearly all my ten reels were now exposed.

The next day we returned to London, and I wrapped my film very carefully in its lead foil. To my surprise, no one zapped it with secret lasers, and it came back from Kodak perfectly developed. I had forty minutes of film.

Let me add a note about drinks at the British Ambassador's home. On our last afternoon we drove through Moscow, its golden domes ablaze with the setting sun, a light blue mist clinging to the damp leaves of the chestnut trees. High above Lenin's tomb a huge red flag floated in the motionless air, driven by a concealed wind machine. Old steamboats plied the river with thin plumes of dark smoke. I could feel Bella and Sonia, our guides, were very excited. At the Ambassador's house we walked into Knightsbridge twee. Wall-to-wall carpets, fake 18th-century reproductions, sporting prints, and little bits of china. Braying Oxbridge lads and lasses of the diplomatic corps, such ennui in their voices, so locked up in themselves, who called our friends 'The Sovs' with a nasal whine that meant 'plebs', the overbred philistinism of these graduates of Mod–lang and Eng–lit carried from birth in the diplomatic bag. 'They go through your undies. They're old spies, these little Sov maids.'

'Another G and T Freddie.' 'This is Alison, what did you say your name was?' 'I'm sorry, I've never seen your films.' 'A friend of mine loved *The Tempest.*' 'How are you getting on? Of course you've seen more than we have in two years. The Sovs don't allow us to wander, ha ha, it's ghastly isn't it?'

We put on brave smiles as our shy and charming friends stood by bemused. 'Of course this house dates from the 1880s, I had an argument with a friend, who said it was built in the 1850s. What do you think?' This from the Ambassador's wife to Bella.

'I'm afraid your friend is right.'

'Oh, how do you know this?'

'I was brought up in a house like this.'

'Oh how interesting, would you like a whisky?'

I wouldn't blame the Sovs for drawing a curtain around this, I felt desperate. If there are bugs in the lady's underwear you can be sure no one would be any the wiser decoding them. The Siberian manners, the frozen smiles, the tedium. 'Do have a good flight home, you're so lucky to be going back to London, there's absolutely nothing to do here.'

Back home I set up a painting with John Watkiss, which he did in a style resembling Soviet Realism, of five of my friends in British military uniform carrying the red flag.

As I remember, you looked at the Soviet footage and from it came the idea of introducing this other element. When you set up the painting did you have anything in mind, or was it just instinctive?

It was instinctive. My observation of the Soviet Union was so different from my expectation. I came back to a situation where my films were still not shown on the television. In the evenings on the TV I watched the police charging miners with a gusto I never expected to see in this country. At this moment, the '80s seemed more ominous than the '30s, the riot equipment more sophisticated. Above it all Margaret Thatcher's monotone, inciting violent action, misquoting Saint Francis.

IMAGINING OCTOBER

HOME THOUGHTS

Scenario of Repressions: riot police in the streets? Films censored by the IBA? Books seized by customs? Bookshops closed down? Politics of regression through economic idolatry.

The harlot's cry in each high street
Weaves old England's winding sheet.
Step forward into the past that is not,
Into the merrie old land of was.
Fun, Freedom, Democracy, and the Rule of Law.

Market Forces,
Mori Polls,
Audience Ratings,
Best means to crush Effective Expression of independent
conscience.

Ad-men false-imaging politics,
Ad-men false-imaging art,
We think you'll like it.
English Bobbies in an English street
Defend the rights of him they beat,
We think you'll like it.
Where there's muck there's brass.
Censorship of Capital.
Manipulators themselves
Manipulated, and in their
Madness seek to abrogate all value.
Everything.
This is shit but we think
You'll like it.
Boredom, inertia,
Systematic exhaustion of conscience,
Sooner annihilate
Millions with Billions,
Than sacrifice the profit motive.
Ad-men false-imaging
The new British Cinema,
Roll on, Chariots of Fire,
Blake's Albion?
Sublime introspective genius subborned
Into the Race to win the Race,
Playing the Pipes of Mr President.
Where there's muck there's brass.

Crimes against genius and humanity,
History ransacked,
    Promoting poverty of intellect and emotion.

PRIVATE SOLUTION
Sitting in Eisenstein's study
With a home movie camera
Imagining October.
A cinema of small gestures.

The criticism is of the West, there are several minutes of slogans, how did you choose the text?

I wanted to make my thoughts clear to the audience. These slogans read in the context of the film appear subtly different on the printed page, where they are not in context. I didn't attempt to make the film reflect the text. The text disrupts the perspective, and the images play against each other. Narrative is supplied by John Watkiss painting the picture.

The film doesn't take a direct line; it's simpler than that, its didacticism is ironic, the problem is no longer one of opposition, but the fiendishly complicated dynamic of the post-industrial state. Both systems are coping with the problems, problems of inheritance. (Sonia, our Soviet guide, said to me on the last night: 'The Revolution lies buried in Novdevechy cemetery.')

These parallels fuelled *Imagining October*. The very sameness of both societies: the great Stalinist buildings look like the Empire State, or the Chrysler building, but, in Moscow, they are the City Library and University, not Cathedrals of Commerce but Cathedrals of Information. They overshadow the first part of the film, with a monumental gigantism that dwarfs the human, cuts out the sunlight, monumental blunders.

The second part shows the people I met. The children in Baku interested me, they are tangled up in rope which they are using as a harness. In *Ivan the Terrible* they would be soldiers pulling an enormous gun, shouting 'To Kazan!, To Kazan!' Children in harness, creating their own harness.

For the viewer those shots are the ones where there is humanity, where you are saying that beyond all this militarism are people: the young man, the old lady. What was the role of the painter in the film?

John Watkiss would have been an immense success in the Soviet Union. Here there was no immediate outlet for his work, except as an illustrator of comics.

How was the film received?

On the first night at the Lumière Cinema some people resented being spoken to so directly, but apart from that the film created a great feeling of sadness. Of something precious that had been lost, the loss of friendship.

It is a very complex film. The other theme, of course, is the connection between sex and the heroic monumentalism.

Monumentalism is always erotic: look at the Albert Memorial. Monumental sculptures search for the first Adam, the original, the ideal before the fall; they are pre-conscious. Because nothing can be wrong with them, they're dangerous.

Imagining October : Children of Baku

Imagining October

Does your interest in the military have anything to do with your father?

Of course. I was brought up behind the barbed wire of RAF camps; that overshadowed the formative years of my life. I was surrounded by men in uniform all day. I got into uniform myself, I was forced to join the cadets.

Are you attracted by that?

No, but it led to ambivalent feelings. I always wanted to believe the men in uniform were attractive. After all, my father was in uniform. There is conflict there.

Is it fundamental? Is it our nature? Is it my narrative? Old RAF flying jackets, loaded pistols, medals and wartime souvenirs. They became my inheritance. I have never been anti-military in the way that some are, how could I be? My father fought a hard war. He fought Hitler, prosecuting the war with a violence that proved uncontainable. I don't know how to solve that, but without men like my father the war would not have been won! After it was over, he carried on the war. It had destroyed his world. He had many friends who were killed, he laid his life on the line but survived. A terrible sadness invaded his life; at the end he became a kleptomaniac, and stole what he felt had been stolen from him.

It is hard to forgive the belts and whips of my inheritance.

In Imagining October *the aggression is cauterised by the artist?*

Yes, that's how I coped with it as a child.

The painter must be you. I feel, when I am watching this film that you are coping with this reality by recreating . . .

At school I distanced myself from the authorities. I wasn't ducking, I just found it impossible to join in. I stood aside, I formed my own garden. The images of the closed spaces in my films are an attempt to find a safe-house. As early as the age of five I knew I wouldn't join.

Now you might think that I should have got over all of this by now, repaired the fences. But then, why should I? Why shouldn't I invite people into another garden, rather than walk in theirs? Perhaps I might create a locus of calm into which people could walk, but the path was jagged. I think why I like *The Wizard of Oz* so much is that at the end we return HOME, after hazardous adventures. There's no place like the HOME-movie.

The film has that dream-like quality, you start with yourself and call it Imagining October.

The film could have been called *Imaging October*, but I decided on *Imagining October*. It was filmed in October, about an October revolution, Eisenstein's film was called *October*: these were the connections.

We are all accomplices in the dream world of soul; it is not just personal, it's general, we make these connections all the time. As Heraclitus said: 'Those who dream are co-authors of what happens in the world.'

Do you feel that your work has been too negative? Sebastiane, Jubilee, The Last of England. The Tempest *is the odd one out, but there is very little hope in them.*

They are the hope, the activity is the hope. I don't think I should project false hope if I don't feel it. If I had been living in a different time, in a different culture, I might have found more reasons for hope. But I don't think that negativity is negative. I think of myself as an optimist! If I were negative, I would have stopped, committed suicide! I haven't done either of those things yet. It may be painful for the audience to stand with me peering over the abyss, but I was on the edge of the precipice all my life.

I was born with sirens wailing, bombs fell through my childhood, I watched the world militarise, I watched the industrial machine destroy the ecological fabric, I saw the poisons running through the rivers and the forests dying, the atmosphere changing; the whole thing was very very dangerous. Yet I lived for forty 'Golden Years', post-war years. Without—at least in Europe—any actual war or any real disruption. There may have been the odd terrorist, there may have been the decay of the inner cities, but, compared with the problem of living in a poor country, our problems were negligible.

At the same time we were living at the expense of the others, of the planet itself, so that there was always a feeling of guilt. You knew as you went to buy your coffee in the morning and your bread, that you were living better than the kings of old. At ten I'd seen the very extremities of wealth and poverty in Pakistan: the shanty towns made me shudder, I could barely look at them. There are no such problems in Great Britain, just inequitable distribution.

QUISLINGS
The History of the Official British Cinema
by
SIR MICHAEL DEREK ELWORTHY JARMAN

With the collapse of the pound in the mid-'70s, established British film directors moved to Hollywood. The cinema of social ruins fell into realism. A few took refuge in television. Into the vacuum came . . .

The Fabricators of the British Film Renaissance.
It was no easier here than the Soviet Union (must be a comic? . . . See Korda). But if you were a bright advertising executive, it was all mapped out for you. You'd move into the centre, with your old chums from the *agency*, and buy your place in the *Sun*. The *agency* had bought the government for the people, or was it the other way round? So it was easy for them to buy you anything. After all they had bought the *greatest modern art collection in the world*, so why not buy a *renaissance*? Get on *the boards, the board of the Film School, the board of the Tate Gallery*, accept any *board* going.

YOU WERE THE CINEMA. The *press* said so. But the *British cinema* could be a millstone, as well as a stepping-stone. It was, after all, 'over the garden wall', so muddled that it was only interested in *Oscar winners*, so you waved the *flag*, your *flag*, and convinced them it was theirs. They all clapped.

The British Cinema was now the property of absentee landlords, on a 'plane to *Hollywood*. 'We are living in an international situation.' The old guard had left the field

The Last of England

clear, they had stayed there (your secret ambition) making *American* product; you would be more subtle; you would make *American* product here, and convince them it was *British*. As everybody on Wardour Street was on the gravy train (Concorde), you could not be discovered. Of course you needed directors, assistant directors for your projects, what were their names? You've forgotten them already.

Your product, some muscular *Christianism* and jingoism, crypto-faggy *Cambridge* stuff set to William Blake's 'Jerusalem'—a minor poet who wrote this popular football hymn. Lots of running nowhere in slow motion, truthfully reflecting the *climate*, none of these people had anywhere to go, they had 'arrived' by covering the smallest distance with the biggest noise to the *Royal Command*; you reflected this. Oh, the *renaissance*, I nearly forgot; some of your chums sponsored a *Revolution*, and lost the *renaissance* with it. That hurt a little, but who cares, it was another little fiasco over the garden wall, and you were busy re-writing history, far away in *Hollywood*.

SQUAD SQUAD 'SHUN . . .
   SQUAD AIM . . .
      FIRE ★★★★ ★★★★ ★★★★ ★★★★ ★★★★ ★★★★ ★★★★ ★★★★
WHAT SHALL WE DO WITH THIS ONE SIR MICHAEL?
THE LIME PIT, HARRY.
NO MARK, SIR?
NO MARK, HARRY.

�֍ III ֍

MAORIS

I looked at a photograph of my father and his three sisters, and it struck me . . . (maybe it's just physiognomy changes through the generations) that these Edwardians had . . . that the sisters looked like . . . Maoris. So for a while I went around boasting I had Maori blood.

One day I plucked up courage, and said to my father: 'Do we have Maori blood in the family?' He was speechless, he was so shocked, I don't think he had ever expected this question. After a moment he said: 'Of course not! That's preposterous.'

So I said: 'Is there any way of looking back through the records, in New Zealand?' 'No,' he said, 'all the records were burnt late last century.'

To save the situation I changed the subject to St Germain, the Saint in the family, St Germain, patron of Parisian night-life.

AN INHERITANCE

I was born on the 31st January 1942 at 7 in the morning, in Royal Victoria Nursing Home, Northwood; a late Victorian suburb of London, where my grandparents had retired after a life spent in the tea and timber trade in Calcutta. My father, a young RAF officer, met my mother at a dance at Northolt airfield in 1938. She was 20, he in his early 30s.

My father second left, my grandfather and grandmother

My father had lived in this country for ten years. A second generation New Zealander, his grandfather had left the family farm in Uplowman in Devon late in the 19th century, to farm on the Canterbury plains near Christchurch. He had been brought up on the farm, riding the 25 miles to school and back each day; as he made the journey he dreamed of becoming an engineer, and, as opportunities in New Zealand were limited, sailed for Britain in 1929 with the idea of staying four years. Except for two brief holidays, he was never to go home; he was to make his life in this country. His marriage and the advent of the war put any possibility of returning out of the question, though I know he always dreamed of the plains, and hardly a day would pass without some echo from the mysterious world of my antipodean uncles and aunts.

It was a cold and foggy day when he arrived at Southampton and boarded the train for London; London seemed to him dirty and rather inhospitable. After searching unsuccessfully for a cheap hotel he spent the first night at Toc H, Kennington. The next day, after checking in at New Zealand House, he went to the Air Ministry to enrol for the RAF. Any illusion that the old country welcomed its colonial sons was quickly dispelled, as the officers who interviewed him seemed preoccupied only by the fact that he might return home. He recorded that his reception was as frosty as the weather. Surprised by this attitude and disillusioned with the metropolis, he took digs in Watford which he described as 'a quiet leafy suburb'. He received his commission.

When he died last November, in the magpie jumble of his home there were over 200 letters describing his RAF life and neat files recording his search for his roots in

Devon. He was obsessed by a need to belong. Few of the locals in Lymington could have guessed that the Air Commodore with his monocle was a New Zealander. For my father became a chameleon. In order to beat the British Establishment, he joined them outwardly, but inwardly rejected them. He fought their war mercilessly and felt cheated. He bought me a private education, but I could tell he hated the public school ethos. He turned me into what he most loathed: an Englishman, with an accent he adopted but despised. To make sure neither my sister nor I forgot this sacrifice, he catalogued and filed every school bill, and never forgot to tell us how much we had cost him.

Back in 1938 my grandmother met the handsome young squadron leader for the first time. He arrived with a Siamese cat, which eyed her pet canary, leaving it severely disturbed: their relationship got off to a bad start. My mother was very beautiful, and although my father could hardly be termed a gold-digger (the family had little money, as my grandfather had died very young) my grandmother disapproved of him. She was not a snob—the dislike was instinctual. However, my mother won the day, and married him under a bell of daffodils, at Holy Trinity Church, Northwood in late March 1940.

The wedding photo appeared in nearly every national newspaper. A year and a half later telegrams congratulated them on my arrival—from the First Lord of the Admiralty, and the Air Chief Marshal. My parents sent out a card, a drawing of me in a spitfire. Welcome Pilot Officer Derek Jarman and congratulations.

My father was a keen amateur photographer and cineaste, and I make my film debut in my mother's arms in the garden of a house they rented at RAF Wittan: I

My father 1939

My great-great-grandfather on the farm at Uplowman

have used this at the end of *The Last of England*.

Do I remember my childhood through the 40 minutes of this film and hundreds of photos? Or do I have memories I can disintangle? My first memories are, strangely, a magic lantern with a dozen or so slides, some of which were broken; and a wind-up gramophone playing Paul Robeson's 'Lullaby' and my mother singing the Skye Boat Song in the kitchen. Before we moved to Italy when I was four, I remember only Grandmother Mimosa's flat, its pearl-grey walls, and peach mirrors, antimacassars, and pink satin tablecloth with the cut-glass cruets. Later when we returned from Italy, I remember my first dialogue. 'These are cornflakes. They're very special. We used to have these before the war. And this is a banana, Derek.' Grandma worried if you forgot to dry between your toes, and allowed us to watch her making up at her table with its diamond-faceted powder-jars, amber beads, and blue birds, which flew for luck across the mirror between the silver portraits trimmed with eidelweiss and mimosa.

'Deki' was her favourite; and she protected me with increasing short temper from my father's outbursts, which grew more severe as the war continued. Many years later the RAF psychiatrist told my sister that all the Pathfinders have severe psychiatric disorders. Back then, returning from another raid on Stavanger or Cologne to a screaming baby, tempers frayed, the wartime aggression flared; and this carried on through the peace to the third generation, as the family became an extension of the war.

This was never so evident as when my father drove up to London. He demanded complete silence, and treated other travellers as the enemy. 40 miles an hour he went up the motorway and down Oxford Street. Perfect for the engine, he said, our lives depended on it. 40 mph was the most dangerous speed: one moment we were crawling like a snail along a motorway, the next careering down some High Street. He had the wartime reputation of never avoiding the flack: he just flew straight ahead steadily. I believe he terrified his crew. He was determined we notice him, pay respect. My sister and I would pass through the rules of the day: no more than four inches of water in the bath, two sheets of toilet paper. He was determined to impose austerity, all luxury was forbidden. It's the classic fag's father. Thank God they exist, and thank God I had one. After all, childhood only lasts to puberty, then one has the rest of one's life to enjoy oneself unravelling the damage. It's the most distressing sight to see happy families, nothing good can come to them. I cherish the moment when, over the kitchen sink, my mother said to my father: 'Thank heavens our children are not normal, they are so much more interesting than their friends.'

But I regret him, poor soul, in his old age eating baked beans and boiled eggs; alone in his fortress home, leaving a miser's fortune that would have made my mother's life more bearable, especially the last 18 years during which she was dying of cancer. After she died in 1978 we sat on the lawn whatever the weather, he would never allow us in if we visited him; he served tea and very stale biscuits. His first words when we arrived were, 'When are you returning home?' At his funeral, as the kindly priest talked well of him, I thought: how sad it is that none of us can shed a tear. My more practical sister parcelled up the ashes and sent them back to New Zealand—as we had no idea where he had scattered my mother's ashes, whose only memorial is my film of *The Tempest*.

My mother 1939

My father and his Wellington 1940

THE TERROR IN A PHOTO

My father was disgustingly fit: he sailed for the RAF, taught astro navigation, was an examiner for the master mariner's certificate; at 70 he would take out an ocean-going yacht in a howling gale with a crew of young men in their 20s, and return after a couple of days bright as a berry with all the boys exhausted. From dawn to dusk he would be chopping wood, dismantling cars. When he retired from the RAF and wished to commute his pension the doctors called him back, they were certain he had sent someone younger in his place.

At 65, he had the physical alertness of a man in his mid 40s. He was very proud of this. It was his inheritance. It confirmed the superiority of a country upbringing in New Zealand. It showed the British up for what they were, a bunch of weaklings. My sister and I dreaded those after-noons when he insisted we crew for him. The more the sea crashed over the bows, the happier he was. He always won the race, and if he didn't he blamed us, shouting, 'Not that way you bloody idiot!' At Seaview in the Isle of Wight on those summer holidays I did everything I could to be out of the way, making myself as scarce as possible, which increased his moodiness.

'Why do you think I brought you on this bloody holiday? To sit around and build sandcastles?' Everything about the yacht club was a humiliation: ghastly middle-aged men in shorts, their wives deserted on the verandah, making do. My mother, ill as she was, I think found the sailing a release. It didn't stop with the weather—in mid December he was out in his Firefly sailing on the Welsh Harp through the ice. It gave her time, she liked these holidays by the sea, as she hated the house he designed and built in Northwood. The summer she died she had finally organised her escape, buying a house in Lymington. My aunt said she would have divorced him, but she had no independent income, she was trapped, but never showed it. I never saw a shadow.

The cortisone took its toll. She worried a little about her looks, and grew increasingly forgetful; perhaps that's why she left so many little notes for us pinned to the doors, or the refrigerator, when we came home late: 'Don't forget to shut the door', 'Food in the fridge'.

One June evening she was entertaining the editor of the *Daily Mail* and his wife when a large caterpillar crawled from his lettuce and started off round the rim of his plate. She noticed and so did I. It was one of those caterpillars that bunch themselves up measuring the inches as they crawl. Round the plate it went. We carried on talking. Suddenly she said 'Oops' and grabbed it laughing. He didn't see the joke, and left the rest of his salad. Later in the meal she produced strawberries, the first of the season; everyone waited for the big moment and we all tucked in together. There was a long silence: 'Oh my God,' she cried, 'how silly of me, I've covered them in mayonnaise instead of cream.' Then laughing, she took them back to the kitchen to wash them. The drugs played tricks.

One night, when I was seventeen, she came back from a party in London, and took me aside. A very distinguished silver-haired man had come up to her, apologised for the intrusion, and asked her how she felt; he knew she was very ill. 'How do you know that?' 'I'm psychic,' he said. He then proceeded to tell her about herself and the two of us. I was an artist and one day I would be successful. This thrilled her, as by now she pinned all her hopes on

My mother, Pakistan 1953

my sister and me, she lived through us. There was nothing much at home. She kept every news-clipping, and came to every opening of the films. At the opening of *Jubilee* she sat in her wheelchair in the aisle. After I'd wheeled her back to the car she said 'It's one of the best movies I've seen. It's so accurate.'

Her life was as open as my father's was closed. All our childhood friends came to our house, everyone was welcome. One afternoon I came down to the kitchen to find her entertaining a black preacher nearly seven feet tall with dreadlocks; he was hell-bent on baptising her with a bottle of cooking oil. She persuaded him not to pour it over her hairstyle and had me baptised on my knees on the kitchen floor instead. She made him a meal, and while she was doing this, my father came back from work in his bowler and monocle, and retreated into his workshop without a word. She was game for anything to liven up the suburban monotony.

It seemed strange that my sister and I never put two and two together, until the week of my mother's death. The disappearances were quite dramatic. My mother unwisely said one afternoon: 'I'm leaving you your grand-mother's pearls' (her most valuable possession); they disappeared without trace. After her death the situation degenerated into a tragi-comedy, as my father switched his attention to his grandchildren. The saddest develop-ment was his treatment of his eldest grandson which reproduced our relationship. Sam was the first to accuse my father. At the age of four, blamed by my sister for something that had been lost, he said quite innocently: 'Grandad took it.' My father flew into a rage and deman-ded a grown-up apology, and from that moment point-edly bullied or avoided the child. Sam never got a birthday or Christmas present, and this was always cruelly emphasised by my father. 'There's something for Kate, but there's nothing for you Sam, and you know why.' If our society condoned patricide, I think both my sister and I would have attempted it. We discussed it half-jokingly over the telephone often enough.

In the summer of 1986 my father had a stroke which left him with no speech and little movement. By a miracle his character changed. When I arrived at his bedside in Southampton General Hospital he broke into a radiant smile. These silent and public encounters were hardly an ordeal. It had never been possible to talk to him. Now both of us talked at him. If there was any meeting of our minds, it was marked by formal silence. He seemed happier than I ever remembered. Perhaps he was always a child who wished to be looked after. He had changed one cell for another: the location seemed of little importance. He sat at the window staring blankly into the road. Back at his home my sister and I sorted through the maddest inheritance. 90 bottles of whisky (he never drank), enough baked beans to fill a kitchen cupboard, 100 stolen cartons of lavatory paper, on and on, drawer after drawer, pens by the gross, envelopes by the thousands. Nothing in the place we expected. I suggested, half-joking, we could make use of a metal detector. In a cupboard I found two presentation photo mounts in leather embossed with the Royal Coat of Arms. My sister suggested taking a photo of my mother which she discovered fitted them perfectly to put by his bedside. When she gave it to him in its stolen mount I have never seen such distress, perhaps we should have anticipated it. It was as if all his secrets had been discovered.

I felt sorry that we had done this, and still worry about

My father attends a dress rehearsal 1953

it. I think in his madness he thought we never knew, though we had played a game of hide-and-seek during those last years. 'You distract him while I go through the boot of the car.' I would start an argument about South Africa while my sister stole the keys. It was amazing what he packed in. Besides his granddaughter's bike (we let him get away with that one) there was the lawnmower, everything but the kitchen sink. I think he gave it all away like some latter-day Robin Hood; I don't think he thought we deserved anything.

After the opening of *Caravaggio* he confided to Tilda proudly, 'Derek has never asked me for anything.' How could I? At moments when I was dead broke, my mother suggested he might help, but he left the room muttering something about standing on your own feet, and of course when I did stand on my feet he hated it: for he lost power.

What damage life wrought on the Air Commodore. He seemed to resent surviving the war; every letter he wrote was a plea to be put into the most dangerous active service, repeatedly requesting to join the Pathfinders; his request was granted but he survived to endure the peace; flying his bombing missions through Tesco and Safeways, perhaps he recaptured the thrill. My grandfather Hedley, a dear old gentleman, visited us one summer; violinist and Chairman of the Tramways of Christchurch, his only ambition was to put a £5 note in the restoration box of every cathedral he visited. As we drove to Lincoln, he missed the lights and my father slammed his foot down on the old man's toes. What a row they had. I wonder what their relationship was. I'm thankful that if these patterns reproduce themselves through the generations, I have brought it all to a halt. It would be easy to say forgive and forget, it would be easy for me to write a sympathetic portrait, I could discover enough reasons to explain it all away; but this is after the fact. A four-year-old hasn't the capacity to understand the vagaries of the world of the grown-ups when they behave like his playmates, or worse than his playmates. It's difficult to knock down a father who is a DFC with a kamikaze mentality, who boxed and sailed for the RAF.

I took his grandson aside, and said 'You know that there are good men and bad men in the world? Some people sadly have to have the bad men as fathers and grandfathers.' I think he understood.

There were, however, moments when the aggression won admiration. One afternoon, famous in family mythology, Dad assaulted a truculent taxi-driver who had menaced him on a zebra crossing. He let fly with unerring accuracy, with his furled umbrella, smashing the man's windscreen. As the taxi-driver, furious, clambered out of his cab, Dad hooked him round the neck with his umbrella handle, and in a stentorian voice barked at the passers-by to fetch the police.

THE ANGELIC CONVERSATION

FEATURE FILM, IN 35MM, 84 MINS, SHOT DURING THE SUMMER
OF 1984,
WITH A SUPER-8 CAMERA.
TEXT: SHAKESPEARE'S SONNETS READ BY JUDI DENCH.
MUSIC: BY COIL AND BENJAMIN BRITTEN.
WITH PAUL REYNOLDS AND PHILIP WILLIAMSON.
A SERIES OF SLOW-MOVING SEQUENCES THROUGH A LAND-
SCAPE SEEN FROM THE WINDOWS OF AN ELIZABETHAN HOUSE.
TWO YOUNG MEN FIND AND LOSE EACH OTHER. THE FILM ENDS
IN A GARDEN.

The Angelic Conversation *is a dream world, a world of magic
and ritual, yet there are images there of the burning cars and
radar systems, which remind you there is a price to be paid in
order to gain this dream in the face of a world of violence.*

Destruction hovers in the background of *The Angelic Conversation*; the radar, the surveillance, the feeling one is
under psychic attack; of course we are under attack at the
moment. In the background of *The Angelic Conversation*
there is surveillance by Nobodaddy.

However, another sequence deals with male dominance
differently; the ritual washing of the tattooed man who
looks like a king or prince, the giver of rings, carrying
his crown, and sceptre. At the time I was thinking of the
Anglo-Saxon poem *The Wanderer*; service willingly
given, not exacted. There is no compunction in the scene.
'He that has power to hurt and will do none.'

What do you think of Tony Rayns's statement? He said it was the nearest thing to heterosexual kitsch!

Well, it is a love story, why should the Devil have the whole fire? If love stories are kitsch, then, yes of course it is! I understand Tony reacting against it; perhaps kitsch is the wrong word though. For me kitsch is 'gloss', yet *The Angelic Conversation* hasn't any of that.

What has the feed-back been like on the film? Because, along with In The Shadow Of The Sun *it is the most difficult for a general audience.*

When it was shown on television I think it had well over half a million viewers; for me that's a large audience. I don't need the whole world. I was exploring a landscape I had never seen on film: areas of psyche that hadn't been projected before. I have seen very few films on male love which are gentle, they usually have a violent subtext—the violence you have to traverse before you make peace with yourself. People batten on failed relationships, murder— look at Joe Orton: the sad fact is that if he and Halliwell had had a successful relationship there would have been no money in it at the box office.

The Angelic Conversation is gentle. There is that hovering, external violence, but at the end of the film it's cauterised by the blossom, which obliterates the radar. The blossom takes over.

Do you remember at the first screening you made for the BFI, they came up to you at the end and said, 'We didn't think you were going to turn out an underground film.' And you said 'This isn't underground, it's my fourth feature film.'

Angelic Conversation

God, yes, it was just like the guy who came up to me after the launch of British Film Year, and said: 'We'll make an alternative festival for films like *The Tempest* at the NFT.' *The Tempest* alternative? Where do these people leave their minds?

Try explaining to them that I don't make underground films, I have never made underground films. I hate all the labelling, the boundaries drawn by the 'communicators', the middle men who sit between the audience and the experience.

I think that if you had made a violent film the BFI would have been quite happy; by making a less aggressive film, it had quite a strong effect, particularly as you didn't let politics intrude.

Making my films is not difficult, funding them is, how they are perceived is another matter, I get so tired of conventional film.

It's a change of heart we're after not a change of policy; centuries of disinformation don't go away at the stroke of a pen.

Watching The Angelic Conversation *I saw you drew on the tradition (perhaps you are unaware of this), a quite similar tradition to Humphrey Jenning, whose films merge landscapes with action in a very poetic evocation of England. Also the Powell films. 'Place' runs strong in* The Angelic Conversation. *At the end I felt it was about England, landscape, sea. Do you see your films in that light?*

Yes. In the short space of my lifetime I've seen the destruction of the landscape through commercialisation, a destruction so complete that fragments are preserved as if

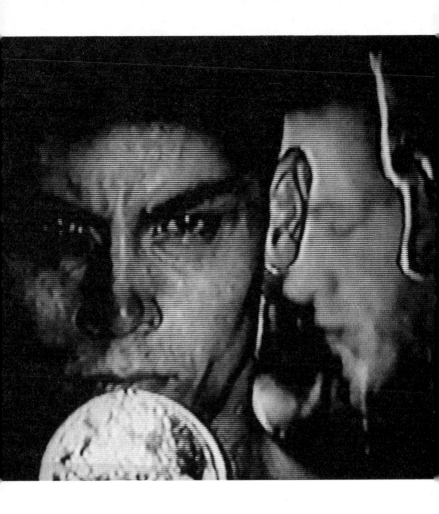

Angelic Conversation: Paul Reynolds

in a museum. You notice this as you drive in the country and enter a 'preserved' area; suddenly there are hedgerows, trees in the fields, and with luck you might see a meadow with buttercups. Down here in the home counties the landscape is blighted. You drive through the small towns and villages which if historic, like Rye, have been made 'historical'—busily manufacturing themselves as picture postcards of their past.

Canterbury is now reduced to an 'historic centre', a heritage town, its barren streets devoid of traffic, taken over by twee boutiques selling superfluous goods. The market town is dead. It is impossible to recapture, walking through Canterbury today, the emotions that fill that last reel of Powell and Pressburger's *A Canterbury Tale*. The city of pilgrims has become an empty 'theme park'.

The land of England was once the home of dryads and nymphs, every now and again you can feel the last of them lurking around a corner: At Dancing Ledge, at Winspit. But much of the land is desolate. Cornwall is a wasteland. Sad Goonhilly with its tracking disks. Land's End.

I am interested in the fact you are the only film-maker in this country who is working on small Super 8 in mainstream cinema. You have a very wide range . . .

I don't want to get trapped! Once a certain type of film becomes identified with you the system demands conformity and forces you to make that type of film; then the films get bigger, your second film bigger than your first, and so on. Till the point when your fifth film is shipwrecked in mainstream, support is withdrawn, and you are unable to work! I can't see the creators of big budget cinema as intelligent, the gigantism seems obsolete, the director's pretention laughable—and also, in a world of diminishing resources, short-sighted, misplaced, and immoral.

Also as you progress in that world, your subjects become limited, your fifth film is always less interesting than your first. It's such an obvious trap. I'm surprised that so many are fooled. I watched a programme about British cinema on Italian television last week; none of the directors seemed to care or even be aware of the context and pitfalls of the world they work in, and, if they were, they studiously avoided making criticism; not one of them questioned anything.

What kind of reception did The Angelic Conversation *get?*

I think this work runs counter to the accepted patterns of sexual politics. But then artists are suspect in that world, we are seen as elitist, and if male, part of the dominant culture. From that viewpoint anyone who picks up a brush or camera is suspect. The '70s propagated the division, successful individuals writing or filming were ostracised, and jibed at. I wasn't one of the 'professionals', my commitment was suspect. There isn't much leeway for part-timers in the cabal; whatever you did it was not enough, the audience wanted everything; as there was so little information they wanted the whole spectrum; of course in 90 minutes that's not possible.

Why is he making his films so difficult? We would really like to see these ideas enter the mainstream in a form like *Dallas* or *Dynasty*, something sensible! There is a deep and pernicious collaboration between camp sensibility and soap opera. I hate the *Dynasty/Dallas* brigade: 'If the world says we are trash, we'll embrace its trash.' For those people films like *The Angelic Conversation* are 'impossible', that's the word they'd use, 'quite impossible to understand'. But that is of course nonsense; I'm not spoon-feeding babies.

The Angelic Conversation *is quite a tough film. You've set it in a pre-romantic period, a tough period, when intellectual debate was at a high point. It has got a tough backbone running through it. Were you aware of that?*

When you are making a film which doesn't have a script, it becomes an extension of your life. It's not sentimental because I'm not a particularly sentimental person, sentimentality doesn't come through. And after all, Shakespeare's sonnets are not sentimental; one of the most consistent feelings conveyed in the sonnets is loss; like Barthes's *A Lover's Discourse*, you have a laser probing emotion.

This is what interested me about the sonnets. They are hardly taught in schools, they are always too difficult. Too tough with himself for the light brigade to look him in the eye. It's tough being in love.

Another thing struck me. The quotation you start the film with, 'Love is too young to know what conscience is, but who knows not conscience is born of love.' The tension between the Super 8's which are love-born, without conscience, and the other films where there is conscience, and not love. You plugged in to something that was very close to home on that.

I think we should print that quote in capitals—it would be an antidote to all this madness.

When you chose the actors for The Angelic Conversation,

Angelic Conversation: Philip Williamson

did they just arrive out of the blue, or did you have them in mind before?

I had seen Paul Reynolds out quite often in various clubs, I thought he had an amazing face, moody with great sadness, he seemed set apart. He was always immaculately dressed.

One evening I mugged up the courage to speak to him, as I was slightly drunk. I said I had always wanted to film him, but I hadn't had a chance, as the years had passed without a film being funded. I thought that he would probably not be interested, but he turned round and said that he must be the only person in the club who had understood the Latin of *Sebastiane*. He was an archeologist, doing a PhD in late Roman pottery. In *The Last of England* he is an archeologist.

We started the film, I had no idea that I was going to make it a love story! The initial attraction was mine for him. This 'love affair' was purely cinematic. Out one evening we saw Philip, and Paul said, 'He looks great.' I said, 'Why don't we put him in the film, shall I go over?' It was a sort of dare! I said 'Let's make the film a love story, because then it will be commercial.'

'You must be joking,' said Paul.

So I went over to Philip and said, 'I am making a film with Paul, and we think it would be great if you were in it.' He said, 'Yes.' I filmed the love affair between them.

The love scene was difficult, as it tied the whole ambient structure together. As long as they never met along the footpaths I could weave figures of eight through the landscape.

We filmed that sequence at home, both in Super 8 and video, our first attempt looked quite wrong, hurried and furtive, so we came back a week later and re-did it.

The fight sequence was one take?

Virtually one take. We didn't rehearse it. The fight
sequence and love sequence were both done in one day.

They gave us the centre of the film. Apart from that
most of the footage with Paul was shot in the Isle of Grain,
to the East of London on the Thames estuary, a very
mysterious landscape, one of the oddest places. The other
material, with Philip, was shot at Winspit and Dancing
Ledge. The house was Montacute House in Somerset, a
very fine Elizabethan mansion.

What about the fan, whose idea was that?

I am fascinated by fans, my mother always carried a fan,
I used to buy them for her. Philip in his black dinner-suit
and black fan becomes the Dark Lady of the sonnets. I
didn't make that connection till after the film was complete. At the same time he is an observer, musing at the
window. The lily-pond is a wishing-well; Philip sees
memory in it at the end of the film.

The Angelic Conversation is a journey of discovery, my
journey of discovery through the summer of '84. After
everything was finished I placed the sonnets in the soundtrack that Coil composed. I had always wanted to make
a film for them. I asked Judi Dench to read them, I wanted
a woman's voice so that there was no confusion. If I had
used a man's voice it would have seemed that one of the
young men was talking about the other. One of them
would have had the dominant voice, and I didn't want
that to happen, so the voice became that of an observer,

Angelic Conversation: the garden at Montacute

leaving the imagery autonomous. It also established the feminine in the film, which otherwise would have been lacking. It completed it.

You seem to connect love with knowledge; this goes back to Greek ideals, where the only true knowledge is one that comes from love. Jubilee *was preoccupied by ignorance, a lack of discovery. The only people who seem to know anything in* Jubilee *are John Dee and Queen Elizabeth. They animate . . . there is a love there that none of the other characters have, they are loveless.*
Whereas The Angelic Conversation *is all about discovery.*

The Angelic Conversation moves through the same landscape as *Jubilee*. Elizabeth and John Dee are wandering along the same cliffs, at Winspit, as Philip.

The new film *The Last of England*, also ends there in the sunset.

THE TECHNIQUE IN WHICH THE ANGELIC CONVERSATION WAS MADE

On the Nizo camera there is a dial which allows one to take speeded-up film; you take single frames, if this is projected at normal speed, it goes fast. But I have projectors which go at slow speeds, so the film is restored to a near normal pace, like a series of moving slides.

I re-filmed the projection with an ordinary Olympus home-video camera connected to a U-matic deck. In order to get unusual colours I fiddled around with the white balance button. Sometimes I put a piece of red paper in front of it, which gives the film a greenish tint, or a piece of green paper, which would give it a reddish tint.

The single frame makes for extreme attention, a concentration that is voyeuristic. Time seems suspended. The slightest movement is amplified. This is the reason I call it 'a cinema of small gestures'.

Does it make it more important to get the right faces? Especially as when they are slowed down they show the slightest flicker of emotion. Could you eroticise Edward Heath's face?

I wouldn't use Edward Heath as an erotic image! But, I think he would make a wonderful abbot. I could see him in Edward II as the Bishop of Winchester. In the right circumstances it might even be possible to reclaim Margaret Thatcher as a sympathetic image—the task would be Herculean, but it might just be possible.

You use facial types much like Pasolini.

Perhaps it is a painter's eye, all Italian film-makers look through painters' eyes.

Is that sexual?

Not particularly. The subject of most painting is the human face or body. This is why Italian cinema has that quality. The film-makers have inherited it, it's in their blood. But it's much wider than that. For instance, in *Caravaggio* when an Italian extra relaxed he relaxed into a classic pose, whereas the English slouched, they didn't

146

Angelic Conversation

define their space. Pictorial awareness is not part of our word-based culture. British cinema lacks this tradition.

The Angelic Conversation *was the film closest to the painted image. Few people know this work. It was made outside the structure and therefore not supported. Does* The Angelic Conversation *have a life?*

It should have, but strangely the BFI haven't made a video deal. It would make a great video. There isn't a 16 mm print either. Which stops it being shown in smaller venues.

It worked well on television.

Yes, smaller films do.

MONET'S GARDEN

Artistic revolutions turn in domestic spaces. Monet's water lilies dancing before my eyes. We are off to Giverny. We've calculated that, if we drive like the wind, we can get there and back by the evening to catch the hovercraft across the Channel. It's late May so the garden should be a paradise. Up and down the long straight Norman roads we go, stopping briefly at Beauvais to see the flying buttresses and dizzy vaults of the cathedral, then on. The sun comes out, we're nearly there and we have just half an hour before we have to return. We glimpse the garden from the road, you can't mistake it. At the door we are stopped by an American lady in a neat blue uniform. 'I'm sorry,' she says 'but the gardens are closed till four for a private function.'

'But we've come all the way from England.'

'Well, you've only got two hours to wait.'

'But we can't afford to, we have to get back to the ferry by 7.00. Couldn't we just peek for a second, just stand at the top of the path, and look down the rows of irises?'

'I'm sorry, it's not possible.'

We didn't bother to argue, just turned home sadly, shut out of the garden. As we passed back along the road Rick said: 'Shall I stop?' 'No it's better not to.' You could see the garden was empty, the reception had not begun. Now we'll never see it, we would have to plan the trip, get the passports out a second time. I've known the garden intimately in my dreams since as a child, mad on flowers, I saw a picture of irises blazing in the sun. The picture is now in Houston, Texas.

I found a second-hand copy of a book *Monet's Garden* published by *Country Life*. The second film I made was called *Monet's Garden*.

Matisse, old and bedridden, smiling in his white jim-James as he cuts out Jazz. On the wall in front of him, a painting by Yves Klein in international blue. Down below in the garden Monet hoeing the borders talking to a Japanese admirer in an iridescent kimono. Of course it's too late for me to build a garden now. You need years and friends to swap the cuttings and exchange little recipes. Aunt Isobel fed her maidenhairs on Earl Grey tea. You know the sort of thing gardeners get up to.

As we left we glimpsed the garden bathed in a golden glow. The magic garden, fatal to enter, don't go there 'cos

Angelic Conversation

it's fallen into the hands of demons. Just dream of it when you see an iridescent kimono.

My own garden in the flats here' hardly ever sees the sun, and its 30 black plastic pots are under continuous attack from bully pigeons who pounce on the flowers. Not one crocus has flowered this spring, all of them neatly scissored by murderous beaks. But it doesn't stop me. Like all true gardeners I'm an optimist.

THE BLUE ROSE

Do you see it as inevitable that you ended up making films? Could you have taken a different path and saved us having to read this book?

Do any of you remember Margaret Thatcher, who started the horticultural race that bankrupted the State of Albion? I met her at the hunt ball in Grantham when I was 11; she saw me in a corner, and asked me to dance. I was terrified: she was only 27, but could have been my mum.

What did we have in common? Not very much you might think, but I was a forward child, so I swallowed my embarrassment and I told her as we danced about my garden; we danced the Waltz, the Military Two-Step, the Dashing White Sergeant, and then the Gay Gordons, then I lost her in the Conga.

But I wasn't to lose her forever; much later she became

Prime Minister and asked me to become Minister of Horti-culture in her fourth, fifth and sixth terms. She said I wasn't wet; well, I knew that! And I shared, secretly, her cherished ambition to find the Blue Rose.

At nights we discussed history, tulipomania in 17th-century Holland, Russell lupins, hollyhocks and mimosa— my grandmother's favourite flower. We had in common a dislike of pinks, both the flower and the colour. She also hated red, as it turned to noise on video (she was keen on video).

Her first request was that every park in London should be planted with flowers of blue: gentians, love in the mist, and delphiniums, and her much loved wisteria. She was pleased with the result, but at night she went home to her little house and in the dark she would be overtaken by sadness when she thought of the Blue Rose.

I tried dying roses with blue ink, like they dye carna-tions; but I didn't convince her: she said she needed a True Blue. So whilst we danced, as we often did, at Buckingham Palace, and Lancaster House, we discussed floral pedigrees. Perhaps I could cross Peace with Hiroshima's Children.

Peace was a horrible flamboyant product of the '50s. I decided to put it in a nuclear reactor, hoping to achieve our secret by mutation. Now I didn't grow just one rose, but thousands—I wanted to be certain. We discussed where we should plant our experiments, she brought in MI5, and the SAS. Strong, able-bodied YOPs signed the Official Secrets Act, and planted air bases and army ranges with roses, hush hush. In the fourth term we invented the Purple Rose, which we called the Royal Rose. We won ten medals at the Chelsea flower show, and Her Majesty graciously accepted a bouquet.

In the fifth term we achieved the Slate Blue Rose, which

The Sick Rose

O Rose thou art sick,
The invisible worm,
That flies in the night
In the howling storm;

Has found out thy bed
Of crimson joy;
And his dark secret love
Does thy life destroy.

Imagining October

My mother, my sister and myself

we christened 'Princess of Wales'. We created a fashion. By this time I was spending the education budget, the health budget, and the entire army was working for me covertly.

In the sixth term, we discovered the perfect Blue Rose, which we called MARGARET. This year we are putting down several million hectares of Margarets in Surrey; it's going to be a fine blue sight. I have bankrupted my country, but saved the service industries.

This goes to show how far a boy who danced with a girl at the hunt ball in Grantham can go.

❧ IV ❧

EVASION

What do you see in those heavy waters? I ask.
Nothing but a bureaucrat from the ministry poisoning the
buttercups with a new defoliant.
What's that I hear?
The sound of Gershwin on his ghetto blaster.
What else?
The atom splitting,
And the whispering?
Half-truths spilling from the minister's case
Wriggling in the sunlight.
What are they saying?
All's well, no comment. Some of them are silent.
Ah here's the guard.
What's the password?
EVASION
What else do you see?
Lies flowing through the national grid, and bribery.
All's normal then?
Yes.
Where's Hope?
The little white lies have carried her off beyond the cab-
bage patch.
They've murdered her?
Yes.
And Tomorrow?
Tomorrow's been cancelled owing to lack of interest.
You saw the graffiti years ago on the Euston Road, and
didn't believe it;
What proof do you need the world's curling up like an
autumn leaf?

The storm's coming to blow it into the final winter.
Can't you feel the days are getting shorter?

THE LAST OF ENGLAND

FEATURE FILM, 88 MINUTES, 35MM, COLOUR AND BLACK AND
WHITE.
FILMED IN LONDON, LIVERPOOL, NEW YORK.
FOOTAGE FROM THE 1920S BY HARRY PUTTOCK, AND FOOTAGE
FROM THE 1940S
BY LANCE JARMAN.
WITH: TILDA SWINTON, SPENCER LEIGH, AND SPRING.
DESIGN: CHRISTOPHER HOBBS.
COSTUME DESIGN: SANDY POWELL.
SOUNDTRACK: SIMON TURNER.
CAMERA: DEREK JARMAN, CHRIS HUGHES, CERITH WYN EVANS,
RICHARD HESLOP.
PRODUCED BY: JAMES MACKAY, DON BOYD, YVONNE LITTLE.

WHAT SORT OF PEOPLE DO YOU THINK
WE ARE? INTERVIEW APRIL 15TH 1987

The Last of England isn't finished, so it's difficult to tell you
what I've made, but I could make a guess. The film is like

Phoenix House. December 1986

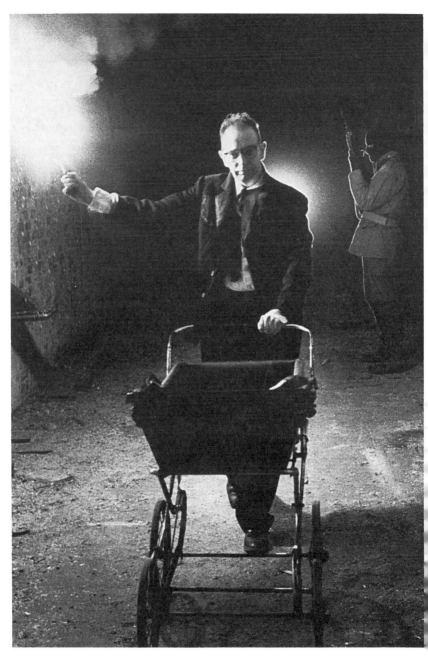

The Last of England: James Mackay, the producer

no other; occupying its own space; usually when you're told this it's a publicity stunt; but with this film it's true; but don't think I feel novelty a virtue. I was quite happy to make *Caravaggio* in a more formal tradition. *The Last of England* is exciting because it makes all recent British Cinema look very tired. It makes the work of my contemporaries pale into conformity.

Whose work?

Greenaway—'Painting by Numbers', Frears—the good craftsman.

Whose work do you like?

Should I like anyone's? I didn't get into this to like or be liked.

But why do you make films?

For the camaraderie. I improvised *The Last Of England*— no script, scripts are the first restraint; the commissioning editor opens the mail and writes his hurried replies: 'Dear Mr Dickens, the script for your new novel *Bleak House* is much too complex.' And how about: 'Dear Mr Britten, I really think we've had too many requiems, though as you mentioned in your treatment they have had an impressive history, the Board doesn't really feel that splicing them with the Wilfred Owen poems is going to be intelligible to the audience'; 'And as for you, Mr Picasso, the plot for the Demoiselles . . . forget it darling! A cult movie.'

After that none of them got made. Some fucker in Hollywood buggered up the 20th century to build a bigger swimming pool. Film directors are a cringing bunch; they shout and scream to cover the fact that their hearts have been stolen.

Back to The Last of England.

Ah, what's it about? About England, a feeling shared with Oliver Cromwell. Let me read you this:

His Highness's Speech to the Parliament in the Painted Chamber, at their dissolution upon Monday, January 22 1654.

1. Who is this that cometh from Edom, with dyed garments from Bozrah? this that is glorious in his apparel, travelling in the greatness of his strength? I that speak in righteousness, mighty to save.

2. Wherefore art thou red in thy apparel, and thy garments like him that treadeth in wine fat?

3. I have trodden the wine press alone; and of the people there was none with me; for I will tread them in mine anger, and trample them in my fury; and their blood shall be sprinkled upon my garments, and I will stain all my raiment.

4. For the day of vengeance is in my heart and the year of my redeemer is come.

5. And I will tread down the people in mine anger, and make them drunk in my fury.

The Last of England

That's pretty mad, isn't it?

Do you read the Bible?

Yes, frequently. The Song of Solomon. Revelation. You can't leave the Bible in the hands of people like the Chief Constable of Manchester; God alone knows what would happen. Since I'm obviously in the cesspit, I've nothing to lose: I'm out to destabilise and destroy. 'The way up is the way down'—that's Giordano Bruno. I think quite a lot of people would benefit immensely from a short stay in the cesspit.

Can you give me any other leads into the film?

There's no narrative, though there is a love story; it's silent. There are no words in a movie camera. Someone put them there late in the '20s. The 'Cinema' was straight-jacketed, it took a nosedive.

It's completely silent?

No, there was an orchestra, or cinema organ for the silents. I have an orchestra. The foundations for Simon Turner's sound track are the Bach Violin Sonatas, and I've written four 'voice-overs': my reaction to the view from this window of a culture riddled with death-watch beetle. Nigel Terry delivers them in a BBC monotone. The sound track is a palimpsest.

4 AM

Imprisoned memories prowl thro' the dark. Fuck it. They scatter like rats in the echo. Ashes drift in the back of the skull. A goblin parts the black velvets with a slant-eyed chuckle. Panic. I blink as he vanishes into the shadows, hint of predatory cat's eyes. The dust settles thick, so by five when I stagger to the freezing bathroom I leave footprints for others to excavate. They say the Ice Age is coming, the weather's changed. A thin yellow pus drains thro' the institutions, mutating malevolent bureaucracies large as dinosaurs, which prowl the pavements of our regressed neighbourhoods.

Citizens stand mute watching children devoured in their prams. Tomorrow the dinosaurs move on. No one ever saw them, invisible as the atom. In the silence of an English suburb power and secrecy dwell in the same house; ancestral gods have fled the hearth. Strange forces are moving in.

It's very pessimistic? You're a pessimist?

Not at all. The act of making the film is the opposite. I'm not cowering in this room, I'm going down fighting, that's optimistic. This is war, it doesn't matter if I lose the battle, someone else will win the war.

Which battle?

The battle for a cinema which grows up and uses the direct experiences of the author like any other art form, and which stands up to the commissioning bodies and declares that experience is the basis for serious work.

The Last of England: Archaeology

I don't quite understand.

Van Gogh: this is the field I saw this day, LOOK! Why does the cinema need anything more than the field? Its obesity is disgusting.

You shot The Last Of England *on Super 8?*

Yes, because the Super 8 camera is free. 35mm is chained by money to the institutions. It could have been shot on 35mm, but economics have gutted mind from the format. My friends, the bluebells are flowering in the woods of Kent—now do you wait for someone to tell you you can film them? They'll have died before you get an answer. A 35mm crew will trample them to death. I can dance through them, throw my little camera in the air, turn somersaults. Fuck the crane and the track.

Thinking of which, I saw something that interested me a lot on my visit to the Soviet Union, in Alexei Gherman's film *Twenty Days Without War*. The camera tracks to reveal small incidents to tell a narrative, which enriches this great film. Here in the west the camera moves only to impress, for effect, never for depth or information.

You're straying.

What do you want me to tell you?

You tell me.

I can't, the film's not finished, you're the first person I've talked to. Later the audience will tell me what I've made. I'll find out in the question and answer sessions, I'll adopt their best guesses.

My own feeling at the moment is as if some mega production were going on off-screen, perhaps life itself, and I'm travelling through, documenting it. The film is a documentary. I've come back with a document from somewhere far away. Everything I pointed the camera at (my fellow cameramen pointed the camera at) had meaning, it didn't matter what we filmed. This film is our fiction, we are in the story. After all, all film is fiction, including the news, or, if you want to reverse it, all film is fact. My film is as factual as the news.

As I look out of my picture window onto the Charing Cross Road, I see the buildings being dreamt on architects' drawing boards. The road itself was created in the late 19th century, it's fabricated. Who dreamed the bluebells? So, if you are making a film, you can point the camera anywhere you want. Everything is to be interpreted, as Beuys said 'Everyone is an artist', and we live in creation.

So you can use any picture to explain anything?

My 90 minutes are the parameter, there are boundaries— God created the world in just so many days of concentrated thought—that's a feat . . It took six months to steal 90 minutes of your time, and create a world that might have happened.

Steal?

Art is theft. The Kine and the Lyre. There's murder there as well. I find it difficult to step back and describe in words what I saw. If I could I would be writing novels, not making films. I'm like the man who first saw the moving

The Last of England: The royal baby

image. The wave is breaking over me. The feeling is so intense I could be found drowned in the front row of the stalls. Perhaps a chance word on the sound track: 'This way to THE EXIT' will save me.

You see, I distrust the written word in cinema, it plays a dubious rôle. Decisions are made on scripts. This is a farce we all enter into, knowing how foolish we are. Directors, scriptwriters; everyone knows that it's a convenience, a ploy. They know the film will bear no relation to the word. If it follows the letter it will resemble one of those painting-by-numbers kits for children. The creators will bring no information. This constricting method dominates the TV. In that world the conventional is always affirmed, nothing's out of place. Of course life is different. Life is full of surprises and often unpleasant ones. I'm thinking positively, the HIV virus doesn't frighten me, I go to bed with it. It frightens those—the others—the junior health ministers, it's rather like school; I'm glad to say, I've left it.

I'm rambling again, but the path's not straight, I've put all sorts of twists and turns into this book, and into the film.

The cinema's finished, it's a dodo, kissed to death by economics—the last rare examples get too much attention. The cinema is to the 20th century what the Diorama was to the 19th. Endangered species are always elevated, put in glass cases. The cinema has graduated to the museum, the archive, the collegiate theatre, and now it's the turn of video. Video ROOLS. *The Last Of England* is an exotic, a hybrid, it's pivotal. One day a restored print will be shown and they will say: 'Derek went crazy for and with the camera in 1986, stirred the lot up with video. Throwing in a pinch of NAM, a soupçon of ADO'—video techniques that were hardly seen on a large screen before then.

The Last Of England has changed the face of my cinema. It's grown into itself, I know that I can stand by this film even if the critics form a firing squad. What comes next hardly matters. I'm happy with it, and all its flaws. I love the flaws, they are the flaws that the Japanese master potter puts into his work. The arbitrary gesture to spoil a perfect shape. I love the moments which are out of focus. 'I've fallen in love with the dust and scratches.'

Is this a new departure?

No. I've always taken a great interest in form. It's part of a painter's training, form and content. Very few film makers do that here. *Jubilee* was structured like a collage created from juxtaposition, it's parochial, too particular, juvenilia, and at times silly. I could be my own best critic. How else could you have made a film with no resources in 1977? My first three films created the 'independent' feature in this country. No one else did so many. They reflected the flawed situation I worked in. Perhaps that's their strength, certainly they didn't win me much of a following with the funding bodies who've starved me of resources. £240,000 for *The Last Of England*, £750,000 for my cinema this decade!! In all I haven't spent a million on all my films yet; I'm proud of that, also filled with fury for those who deal out the cash. I think that's right.

Do you think this will get easier?

I don't expect that to change; it would be foolish to let my guard down after being punished for making *The Tempest* with six years' silence. I can see the fuckers now:

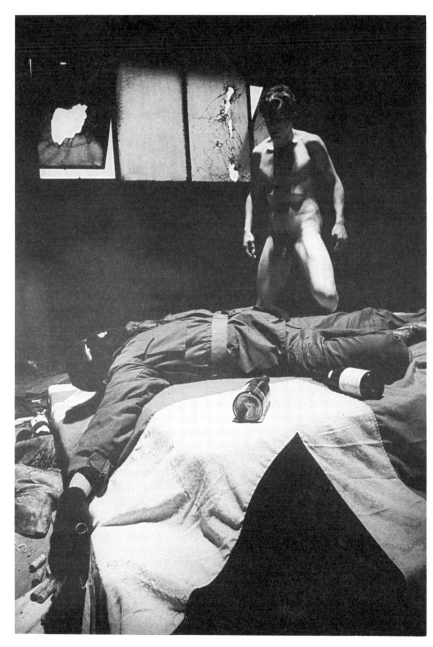

The Last of England

'Well he's uninsurable, probably keel over in the middle of the shoot'; and the sod-awful unions saying 'Well we can't let our members work with him, much too dangerous.'

I don't kiss anyone now.

The past?

The past is present.

Success?

Is there life beyond the department store and the cash register? Now everything is justified in quantities: 30 million watched this one, i.e., the Windsors are a good thing, pull in the crowds, half as old as time itself. They stand like the Colosseum, isolated on the roundabout, while the world roars round; bread and circuses. Nothing alters.

As I made this film I thought even if I throw myself out of the window I'll land somewhere. So I said to everyone 'Jump'. We threw ourselves into the blue, the whole production. We didn't wait for the sunset, just grabbed it.

And how much has it cost?

I'll never know, but it was the film we wanted to make as opposed to the film they would have wanted us to make, and that puts it in a class of its own; it will be finished before we receive a single penny. We gambled everything.

Do you miss the formality of 35mm?

Yes, in a way, but the film world is very old-fashioned. On a film-set the director is called 'Sir'. The ticket-collector at Northwood station used to say 'Good morning, Sir', when I was a twelve-year-old. Making a feature film is like going back to the '50s in the undue respect it pays to the director, and the producer's money. It's a timid world, where a film like *Caravaggio* can be labelled a masterpiece to deflect criticism.

There is an immense hidden censorship. If you are an ambitious young film-maker you work something out within this limiting consensus. You don't adopt a personal view, or, if you do, you do so at your peril.

Could you tell me about the family footage in The Last Of England?

The earliest footage dates from the end of the '20s. My grandfather, Harry, who died before I was born, filmed the family holidays in Bexhill. I have about half an hour of his film. Besides the Sunday lunch, which is in *The Last Of England*, there is tea on the beach, and my mother going back to school. It has amusing title cards so you know who everyone is. Mum is introduced by the card 'ever-smiling Betty'. She is about ten at the beginning, 15 at the end. There were more reels of this film but they were lost by my aunt.

I was so unhappy about this I carried the remaining film away with me on one of my visits home, copied what was left onto video, and never returned the originals. It became a bone of contention with my father in his last years. 'Where's the family movie?' 'Safe and sound', I'd say, and change the subject.

Nothing that belonged to the family was safe, so I knew

The Last of England: RAF Abingdon 1948

I'd made the right decision; and because he knew I loved the film I thought he might destroy it. He'd taken my sister's wedding ring, my stamp albums, his granddaughter's bike—he made away with it by riding it through Oxford at the age of 77. Once in my flat he left nothing unturned. When I was cutting up Physique Pictorials for my theatre designs at The Slade I hid them; I turned my back for a minute to make some tea, and he'd ferretted them out. For months his conversation was loaded with innuendo. He knew too much about my life. Dad barricaded himself in, buried his desires. Living with this 'prisoner' dominated me; eventually he loomed so large he stole my mother's memory, and also, believe it or not, her engagement ring.

Is the colour footage his?

He was a keen photographer, he took his camera up on the bombing raids and was in communication with the air ministry. He shot the footage of the Wellington bombers at Lossiemouth in the film. It's in perfect condition and in colour. His film is about 40 minutes long and starts in 1939 at the World Trade Fair in New York. Back in England he took the camera on his honeymoon. All the wartime footage is shot in the sunlight. Tilda said, 'They don't make summers like that any more.' The Kodak memory has rich colour.

Do you remember being filmed?

No. But the film triggers memories. I see the camouflage, the barbed wire, and the H-blocks of my childhood; my sister Gaye, and myself playing with a ball on the lawns of RAF Abingdon, where my father was Station Commander—I'm six years old, it's the summer of 1948.

THE WINDS OF CHANGE

The sad old Emperor bent beneath his black top hat smiles in the deathly sunlit silence. The Lady next door to me says THERE HE IS! THERE'S HIROHITO AND HIS EMPRESS NAGASAKE. Look! Johnny look! They're playing the funeral march for the Royal Doulton. He stole the patterns way back when you were a boy, no one cared much. They were busy squandering our threadbare patrimony on the atom. Now you see it, now you don't. England had it years back, us kiddies weaned on food parcels from uncle Randy in the wild west, choc-full o' comix and bubble gum. I grew up in the wind of change maam! Quite! Quite blew away my reason. My father's father's father's presentation clock, a black marble mausoleum ticked out my childhood as I died of boredom in my inheritance, 101 years of middle class assurance. The bomb dropped with regular monotony, leaving us waiting—the frosty heart of England blighted each spring leaf, all aspiration withered in the blood.

In the silence of an English suburb power and secrecy dwell in the same house, while far away in the big city the A to Z clamped a grid on despair.

Does the relationship with your father influence The Last Of England *?*

Yes, he created my aversion to all authority, to the extreme patriotism with which he fought the war, which bounced back and destroyed our tranquility. I looked in this poisoned well and saw others celebrating the war, using it to bolster their dominant positions. The dull Windsors laying Remembrance wreaths. All I saw was deceit and

The Last of England

bankruptcy. I hate the voice of my kind, I know who they are, brain-washed in mediocre public schools, brought up to rule over the oiks and wogs. I see through them, God damn them, God damn you all. This country stinks of platitude. The bomb dropped in this child's eye.

Do you see a future?

No.

PROSPERO'S WAND

Last week I broke Prospero's wand, Dee's hieroglyphic monad. I took hold of it silently, shut my eyes for a moment, then smashed it. Seven years, there's going to be a change; I'm coming back with *The Last Of England* and, if I can complete it, *Borrowed Time* will finish the story. I'm looking no further; *Edward II* can wait for the moment, it's just an excuse to cut out sexy Gavestons from magazines.

With *The Last Of England* I've made a journey back of a different sort. *The Tempest* and *Caravaggio* allowed me to form a perspective, to stand back. Now I'm going back to my roots, to lay bare the contradictions. I'm liverish today, have I decided to be ill? There is something terrible in the thought that *I wished this*. Did I have to convince myself that the world could not contain me? I had touched the parameters, could I go beyond them?

The virus produced a quiet space in all the hubbub, achieved a subtle alienation. Dame Perspective, the obsessive mistress. What dark shadows remain to be explored? You only find secrets in the dark, there you can touch them, but they remain hidden, *Nature loves to hide*.

THE LAST OF ENGLAND MAY 3rd 1987

If things had turned out differently much of the atmosphere of *The Last Of England* would have been realised in *Neutron*, a project I worked on from 1981–83. *Neutron* was based on Jung's *Aeon*. Researches into the phenomenology of the self, the self-measured in the life of Christ. The script was a conflict between the active and contemplative life. Topaz, a revolutionary, and Aeon, an artist, meet in a desolate shadowy world, a purgatory where neither of them has an audience any longer. They criss-cross each other's lives in perpetual conflict; at the end we discover they are the same person. It was a very strange script. Based on the Revelation of St John. The angels were a paramilitary group called the Outriders, engaged in mopping up the remains of a world, our world, that had passed away; they relocated it in a bunker where the saved, 'The Saints', cannibalised their captives. The walkie-talkies and intercoms used by the Outriders blasted out biblical quotes: 'You are the first and last, over and out.'

The Last of England: Spencer Leigh wears the heretic's hat

Did you complete a script?

Yes, several of them; all the more formal feature films have been written and re-written; sometimes you feel like a cat chasing its tail, the re-writing is to accommodate possible funding. *Neutron* was a love affair with the shadow, he who walks beside. It ended with Aeon shooting Topaz and becoming HIM; he receives the stigmata, and the world drowns in blood. I was never completely satisfied with the end of the film; it was so important, I couldn't resolve it. I worked on these scripts with Lee Drysdale, a young writer who at the time was a very active member of the WRP. He took on the character of Topaz, and I, Aeon, and we created a battlefield at Phoenix House which lasted for over a year. Looking back I don't think the film could ever have been financed, it would have needed an immense budget. If I had made it I think it would have resembled *Brazil*, a film I really admire.

Neutron *goes back to 1980?*

Yes, to about 1980. I also wrote a medieval script, *Bob up a Down*, and rewrote *Caravaggio* as well as developing my Super 8 films, as the money needed for them was so negligible they were realised. I shot them, then funded them; two were completed in 1984: *The Angelic Conversation* and *Imagining October*. *The Last Of England* is the third film made this way apart from smaller works: *Aria* and pop promos, of which the best is *The Queen is Dead*. This way of working connects me with my original roots as a Super 8 film-maker. DIY school of home movies.

The key to developing this work was the music video which was a phenomenon of the late '70s and '80s, and the expansion of video facilities to service the explosion. These video facilities in London are as sophisticated as any you'll find in the world. By the early '80s it was possible to transfer Super 8 footage to highband, edit in video, and re-transfer the lot back to 35mm film, the gauge of the feature. You could achieve effects on video which would have cost a fortune on film, and all the time the technology was improving; it was impossible to tell now if the image on your TV was generated in Super 8.

Blown up to 35mm, the quality is something quite new, like stained glass, the film glows with wonderful colours. The video gives you a pallette like a painter, and I find the result beautiful. Most 35mm looks pretty hard and brassy in comparison. The system produces blacks like the lead in stained glass, shadowy and mysterious, even when the sun is blazing. Much of *The Last Of England* seems to be filmed at sundown, Eliot's violet hour.

How does The Last Of England *relate to music video?*

The music video is made within a very strict code; people outside the business don't know this—this control goes even to the extent of regulating the colour in case Joe Public thinks his set has gone wrong!

Promos are essentially advertisements, limited glitzy work going for effect. Their chief characteristic is quick cutting; however, they could be the most vital new language, re-introducing the silent image, with an emphasis on style. Style left movies as the generation who grew from theatre through the silents and talkies died. Any old film, no matter how banal, has a visual polish that puts the post-television cinema to shame.

The Last Of England works with image and sound, a

The Last of England

language which is nearer to poetry than prose. It tells its story quite happily in silent images, in contrast to a word-bound cinema. I watch the new crop of British films and smile at their authors' claims. What have these sit-com writers (who can barely grope their way past the TV) got to do with cinema? And those responsible for visualising them, where ever did they learn their language? In some blind institute.

There are very few film-makers of my generation who can pick up a pencil, and probably fewer of them can pick up a camera. It's all rather sad. Of course one can hardly blame them, there is no premium on originality, it will only hold you back. The spoon-fed audience gets its pre-dictable kicks. There's so-and-so's TITS, with the theme song from last year's boring no one band.

Don't worry you'll recognise everyone in the bit parts so no one is going to surprise you, the acting is superb all the way through, no one will reach any depth to disturb you, and even the worst moments will be nullified by British humour which calls a fuck a bonk.

You think this is a film for the '80s because of the nature of the language?

Pop promos have created a new audience, particularly in public places like bars and clubs, where people sit all night watching quite happily. It's a more public entertainment than the TV, a new visual language has been created. *Absolute Beginners* tried to capitalise on this, but the narrative fought it, and it didn't quite work.

At least one critic said that Absolute Beginners *was an endless pop promo. If someone said that of* The Last Of England *what would you say?*

It would be great. The problem was *Absolute Beginners* wasn't a promo, that was rather aggravating. The end credits had the list of characters from the book as long as your arm—you'd glimpsed them but never met them, many major characters reduced to a minute's appearance; it would have been better if Julien had abandoned them. *The Last Of England* is structured in a very different way: dream allegory.

In dream allegory the poet wakes in a visionary landscape where he encounters personifications of psychic states. Through these encounters he is healed. *Jubilee* was such a healing fiction, it harked back to *Pearl* and *Piers Plowman*. Which was also a socio-political tract. In *Jubilee* the past dreamed the future present. *The Last Of England* is in the same form, though this time I have put myself into the centre of the picture.

Here the present dreams the past future. I wrote no script, it is held together by the presence of the author. The audience should be able to 'read' the film fairly easily. This man is destitute, this is a marriage. Its structure suggests a journey: pages turn in a book bringing with them new turnings in direction, building up an atmosphere without entering into traditional narrative.

IMPERIAL EMBERS

The wind blows from the east bringing an acid hail that falls from the leaden sky. The air stutters tic tic tic tic, rattle of death-watch beetle on sad slate roofs. The swan of Avon dies a syncopated death. Ashes big as snowflakes fall, a black frost grips July by the throat. We pull the velvet curtains tight over the dawn, and shiver by empty grates. The household gods have vanished, no one remembers quite when. Poppies and corncockle have long been forgotten here, like the boys who died in Flanders, their names erased by a late frost which clipped the village cross. Spring lapped the fields in arsenic green, the oaks died this year. On every green hill mourners stand, and weep for *The Last Of England*.

The film starts with Caravaggio's 'Profane Love' and is called after Ford Madox Browns' 'Last of England'; are these paintings used for inspiration or to point a direction?

The first third of the film is truly ambient; I carried a Super 8 camera with me from August to October. Working most of the time with Spring, who came with me to America where I was doing the publicity for the launch of *Caravaggio*. The film was an extension of our lives as we travelled around. He hated the *Caravaggio* film and thought my film-making pointless, loved *Dynasty* and *Dallas*, everything I couldn't stand. The relationship was very abrasive. Christopher Hobbs who had painted the 'Profane Love' gave it to me for him to kick to pieces. It seemed a more constructive fate for the picture than ending its life in the Museum of the Moving Image.

After something like 200 interviews for *Caravaggio* I was in a terrible state. It was not just the agony of getting the film made; after it was finished it hung round my neck like the albatross.

Interviewers continually told me I had made a self-portrait. I decided that in *The Last Of England* the autobiographical element should come right to the fore.

So the film starts in Phoenix House late at night, with Spring disrupting my thoughts. He looks and acts like the wicked cupid. A 12-year-old with his finger up his arse.

Today Caravaggio would be immortalised in the tabloids. Even at the time, the painting was hidden behind green curtains (I wonder what Kraft Ebbing would have thought of that). Spring kicks the painting and masturbates over it. It's a love/hate relationship. Meanwhile I'm filming and this is not a passive camera but a cinematic fuck, my shadow falls across him.

It is a very true analysis of the work, in fact much nearer than I got with *Caravaggio* where that had to be fudged; naked 12-year-olds are not a British cinematic speciality. *Caravaggio* boys bring with them a hint of panic, they seem goat-like.

And what about the Ford Madox Brown painting?

Ford Madox Brown came late. I originally called the film 'Victorian Values', but I was told there was a glut of plays with the title. Then came 'The Dead Sea' suggesting Boecklin crossing the waters to the Isle of the Dead; we decided this was too poetic. 'GBH' (Grievous Bodily Harm) seemed a better idea. Suddenly one day I remembered the painting of the emigrants leaving the white cliffs behind for a life in the new world. My great-grandparents

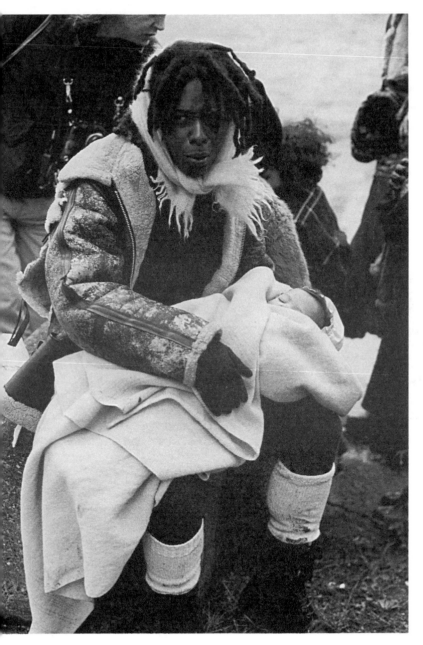

The Last of England

The Last of England

had done that. Left their farm in Middle Combe, Uplow-man, Devon, to go to New Zealand. I have an extraordi-nary picture of them taken in the 1850s. I decided on *The Last Of England.*

Did you recreate the painting consciously?

No, the title came after we had completed the shooting but there are strange coincidences in the sequence with the refugees at the quayside. There is a girl with a plaid scarf who echoes the girl with a shawl in the picture. You your-self noticed the cauliflower which echoes the cabbages in the painting.

Do you think those stuck in your mind?

I hadn't looked at the picture since I was a child, still haven't. But the Victorians, blessed with new methods of reproduction, made images that really stick: Millais's 'Blind Girl', Ford Madox Brown's 'Work', Watt's 'Hope'. If you set me the task of recreating these paintings blind I think I could surprise you.

The Last Of England is not as manipulative as a conven-tional feature; you know—jump here, be frightened here, laugh. Traditional features manipulate the audience. Apart from being stuck with my film for 85 minutes, my audience have much greater freedom to interpret what they are seeing, and because of the pace, to think about it. I have my own ideas but they are not the beginning or the end. The film is the fact—perhaps in the end the only fact—of my life. When I made Caravaggio's life I concentrated on the paintings, not the reported opinions and gossip of the biographers. The paintings were his life, my life is now my films.

I learn an immense amount from audiences. I can go backwards and forwards across a shot 30 times and then see the film another 20 or 30 times and still miss things. For me the voice of the audience is interpretive, teaching me what I have done. I don't work for a passive audience, I want an active audience. I think anyone who works with any degree of commitment will find they want this audience. It's quite small, but it would be greedy to want the whole world. I leave this to those high on statistics. In any case audiences are much more adventurous than is given credit. About half a million people watched *The Angelic Conversation*.

Is the love scene a deliberate echo of the earlier scene with the 'Profane Love'?

It could be seen that way. Though I hardly think a painting makes a successful object of desire. And the sex scene—I don't think of it as a love scene—has a drunken impotence about it which I like; safe sex can be awfully drab if you've experienced sodomy. I'm not certain that I want comfortable sexual encounters, deep down it all seems too cosily suburban and fits too nicely—that's the right word—into the chintzy Englishness of it all.

The sex in my life has been hamstrung. Like a lot of us I'm being good against my better instincts. At first I thought: put up affirmative images; but then I'd done that in the scenes in *Sebastiane* and *The Angelic Conversation*. I don't want to be too precious and protective. The blind drunkenness of the disco seems right. The very negative qualities of disco are brought to the audience's attention in that sequence. The sex sequence is a hangover.

The Last of England

The boy in his suit has stepped out of *Another Country*. He looks like Burgess or Maclean. The terrorists in *The Last Of England* are the establishment. He's a collaborator. The fuck doesn't go well. He ends up smashing the drink bottles, violently rejecting it all. The terrorist is a woman; but the uniform reads the other way. It's a trick.

I connect it with the trampling of the Caravaggio.

It's an embrace to death, kicking blindly, destroying without purpose is endemic to our culture, sanctified progress. Denying value to anything that can't be consumed. I feel this acutely as I get older. The valuable is so fragile. This is not necessarily a painting; it's the environment, the hedgerows, a corner shop, something that you have grown accustomed to and need; suddenly its gone and you ask yourself why. Caravaggio for me was no antique painter; in the 'Profane Love' he's showing this destruction. Creating this wicked angel, a grin all over his face; he's a catalyst, like Terence Stamp in Pasolini's *Theorem* who disrupts an ordered world. Spring, who mirrors this cupid, rejected the ivory tower of my films, he loved adverts and fast food, Campbells soup, *Dallas*, James Dean posing around in that endlessly dull film *Giant*. Turning MTV on and off, he created panic, a flicker film.

Why did you put yourself in the film?

I think film-makers should bring much more of their experience to their work than they do. I've never understood why so many are content to be transmitters of the second-hand. It's epidemic in our film culture. I've always admired Cocteau's *Testament*. It's one of the bravest failures of the cinema. Wells worked that way, and Pasolini; they suffered for it. I heard that Pasolini directed *Salò* in immaculate suits while he put the cast through every imaginable degradation. The film was about exploitation and Pasolini had the courage to identify himself with the seedy manipulators. I think it takes some courage or foolhardiness to put yourself on the line in this way.

It was terribly misunderstood, the audience I saw it with in Paris were scandalised, even now the film is hardly shown. Camden Council attempted to stop it at the Scala a few weeks ago. I've never been convinced of the good intentions of the 'right-ons'.

I would never say I am making this film for an audience: that's very dishonest. It would be true to say I am making this film for myself with my collaborators, we are the community. I am the pivot who gathers the communal threads and creates the pattern, I pull some strands, leave others. The work is the end—whether it's appreciated or not by an audience is not important. The important thing is the creation of the work itself, not the finished product. This harnessing of everyone's creativity, so that when you call 'wrap' for the last time you can all feel the loss physically. Audiences are after the fact.

How did you cast the film?

There was no casting. It happened quite spontaneously, we didn't worry if someone didn't turn up. Spring vanished a third of the way through, he decided to stay in the States. I rang up Spencer Leigh, Gerusalemme in *Caravaggio*, and we carried on the second half of the film which was more structured. We created a formal shoot at the Victoria Docks for a week in November and

The Riverside at upper ground

improvised within it. By this time I had several cameras on each scene; sometimes the people turned up. If not, I got on with it. Sometimes the cameramen got bored and wandered off with some of the actors. The location was pretty spectacular. You could get lost quite easily in the hundreds of derelict rooms. I gave as few directions as possible. Most of the scenes directed themselves.

The wedding was easy, I just asked Mike Laye who was taking the photographs on set to step in front of the camera and improvise a photographic session. He did it brilliantly, I didn't say a word, just filmed as it all happened at breakneck speed. The Super 8 has a wonderful depth of field. No one goes out of focus, you don't have to worry about tape measures. There is a great sense of freedom, you can move where you want to when you want to. It would be quite impossible to recreate this sequence in 35mm. Most of the cuts you see on screen were in the camera. We did very little editing.

Where else did you film?

In Rotherhythe, near my old studio at Butler's Wharf that burnt down seven years ago. I filmed *Jubilee* in the same streets ten years ago. Since then I've often walked along the river past my beautiful studio in the warehouse on Bankside which was demolished for redevelopment, back to Butler's Wharf at Tower Bridge. Bankside's a wasteland now, only the Anchor pub survives; it fronts a brick and concrete river wall pushed into the Thames by the greedy developers. Horseshoe Alley with its cobbles and sombre brick walls has gone; in its place a tangle of nasty reinforced concrete surrounded by barbed wire. Four forlorn designer trees in a handkerchief of grass are the only visible sign of 'improvement'. Everything else is destroyed.

Cannon Street bridge has been put in a concrete straight-jacket, gone are the great Doric columns that emerged like a sunken Temple from the Thames; even the fragment of the old priory has been done over, and its oriel window incorporated into the brick of a corporate fortress.

Butler's Wharf is undergoing the same improvement. Further down, the council estates have been scrubbed and privatised and a sea of folksy little houses invade the gutted wharfs. The old warehouses have been transformed into the most expensive riverside homes.

After this there are miles of desolation with the odd post-modern office building. Beckton with its ruined industrial complexes is one of the eeriest places, like a mammoth silent movie set, its buildings dynamited into the craziest angles. Much of the film was shot on these locations: the old Spillers buildings at Millenium Wharf, the Royal Victoria docks, and of course Liverpool—where the '60s housing developments have proved so hostile to the inhabitants. I gave the desolation continuity in the film by relating it to the camouflaged married quarters at RAF Abingdon with their garden fences topped with barbed wire, and RAF Lossiemouth with its H-blocks.

At our formal shoot at Millenium Wharf we had four cameras: Cerith Wyn Evans, Richard Heslop, Chris Hughes and myself. We had lighting, caterers and a costume and props department run by Christopher Hobbs and Sandy Powell who worked on *Caravaggio*. James MacKay—the producer—did a brilliant job co-ordinating all this; we didn't plan much, just sorted it out as we went. I never knew whether the actors would be coming down or not. Tilda was working on another film; she came down on our last Saturday and we filmed all her sequences in

The Last of England: Tilda Swinton

a couple of hours. For that brief week we formed a tight community. There was no wasted time as we found so much to do.

You talk quite a bit about community.

As a forces child I didn't come from a recognisable community, though I expect forces children could fill a sizeable provincial city. At the Hamburg Low Budget Film Festival last year the workshops talked about community film-making as the only valid form. What if you don't come from their community? Forces children regard the local community as quite foreign. Look at the barbed wire at Abingdon again; as a child I had to pass that every day to go to the town. If you lived on an RAF station you were separate: it was hardly a stable community—we moved every 18 months.

Was the original title 'The Dead Sea' the signpost to an imaginary symbolic landscape?

Yes, it was. I mentioned Boecklin, but Poe was also in the back of my mind, the 'Dead Waters' that lap ominously through his stories. After we had looked at some rushes, Tilda, exhilarated by the film said 'I think "The Dead Sea" gives quite the wrong impression.' I changed the title.

Holman Hunt's 'Scapegoat' springs to mind.

'The Scapegoat' was tethered by the Dead Sea.

SHE

'Everything the anima touches becomes numinous, unconditional, dangerous, taboo, magical' C. G. Jung.

Where is the feminine in *The Last Of England*? Until Tilda takes over the film in its last minutes it is represented by my mother, Elizabeth Evelyn; she picks me up and holds me in the air, to the sound of bombs dropping.

The air-raid sirens still send a shiver through me, something that those born after '45 will never experience. The bombers which flew over my pram became the low-flying jets that rattled the cups as they flew over the married quarters, so low they sent little rivulets of sand running down the sandcastles I built in the sandpit at the bottom of the garden.

In the last minutes of *The Last Of England*, Tilda blown by a whirlwind of destruction, becomes a figure of strength; she is able to curse the world of the patriots: 'God damn you, God damn you all.' She projects and protects love's idyll, a mother, my mother.

HE

'Jung sometimes discusses homosexuality as anima identification' James Hillman.

My mother fought a subtle battle to protect us from my father's irrational outbursts, a weak and absent father who compensated for his inability to communicate with displays of temper. Is this enough to explain a disposition? I think not. If by starting with negative parental images you ended with a child who experienced life in a grey unwelcoming limbo, the case might be argued. The disposition is not a reflection of my childhood, or the disposition of the lads you see happily sizing each other up. Once in bed they are quite at home together. Most likely, they are measuring the size of their dicks, they are measuring up.

THE LAST OF ENGLAND – JUNE 20th 1987

Now you've finished it what sort of things do you think can be said about the film?

It's difficult to talk about it with precision, it's a film which works by evoking memories; these will be different for each person, the film is illusive.

Someone this morning described a sense of déja vu they experienced watching it.

We all star in the home movie, we all played football with our mums, had lunch on a beach, we all got married and christened, everyone of my generation experienced the war.

The war footage is particularly eerie.

That's because it is your life, you will have watched a hundred and one war films. You are never allowed to forget it, so you'll be prepared for the next one.

There is a peculiar intimacy, a naturalness in the film which one would never get from official footage.

My father was an enthusiast, not an official photographer. The war footage lacks an element of propaganda; it is out of context in my film.

Has the content of your film broken new ground?

I think the film has broken new ground, although it's difficult to claim it unless other people follow. Perhaps I've put up a flag on a desert island. I hope not.

There must be a lot of projects never realised that are memorialised somewhere in the film.

Yes, the two soldiers dancing in the yard are from *Salò*, I wrote a small script on Pasolini.

Let's talk about Tilda. What happened during the filming of the dance?

The voice-overs that Tilda made for the film were done when I wasn't there, they were her reaction to the footage when Spencer is shot: she says 'Do you remember?', 'Don't be sad', and at the end she did the same thing, she broke down and cursed: 'Damn! Damn! Damn!' The

The Last of England: Spring

scene is ecstatic, she is the divinity who wipes out memory, all the elemental forces are unleashed in Tilda's dance. The wedding is a marriage of the dead, the child born of the marriage is suicide.

What about the beginning and the end: Spring at the beginning and Tilda at the end.

Yes, Spring is in a cul-de-sac, adrift, his feet are not on the ground, he's a destructive force. Whenever you see him he is hell-bent on destroying: you see a workman laying tar, hammering, making something, then you cut to him smashing windows, wrecking the landscape, fouling the nest. The destruction of the painting was important, Spring reproduces its assault. Caravaggio was unleashing animal passions, that cupid is destructive; Spring is a sly cupid destroying Caravaggio in his turn: destruction is destroyed. He's flying, he's another faery.

The film travels from one psychological state to another, even its ambient structures didn't stop that, it recalls things that happened to us all: my generation's trip to America and all that that implied, the escape from our ruined back yard, the trip back in time with the family, the inherited terrorists, the assault on institutions like marriage, the workmen building prisons for us (the houses in Liverpool are built behind barbed wire). Around the corner lurks a destroyer, who can be unleashed at any moment: the aggressive morris dancers carrying little sticks with which Spencer is smashed to the ground; like 'Gulliver', he's a sacrifice to *Little England*.

There is also an evocation of another painter, Goya: Spencer is dressed as the heretic who's garotted in 'The Disasters of War'. In the City, Jill as Babylon turns the globe: she's the dynamo of the city, the city is on fire, her hands grasp the world, she's spinning it off its axis. Where in all of this is LOVE? Well, love is born in Spencer's execution. It is the first tender moment in the film, apart from the earlier moment of the home movie in the garden. The centre of the film is very dark, unforgiving, like *Salò*: with the refugees from *The Last Of England* waiting on the quay; are they leaving for a new life; or are they going to their deaths? There is an interlude, a moment to collect one's breath as time rushes by in the time-lapse sequence of the empty docks.

The final part of the film brings us back to a world much closer to the present: the destitute tramp is crucified by the recurring images of advertising—American Express Card, Visa Card—the necklace of zircon—in the background the born-again appeal to God; all of this is intercut with a business man in a bowler hat and calipers pouring away grain, the staff of life.

Both those characters show poverty.

Poverty of the imagination; Gerard—with his bowler hat—is a tragic figure. There are continuous appeals on the soundtrack for job creation; when you hear these you see images of the paramilitary: it's very desolate.

The film presents many different agents of destruction: all the forces of Babylon, of consumerism . . .

The film is an attic; I've opened the doors. Think of the mead hall in *Beowulf*, with the swallow flying through: an image I have already evoked in the book. Think of that mead hall full of the junk of our history, of memory and so on; there's a hurricane blowing outside, I open the doors

208

The Last of England: Gerard McArthur

The Last of England: Spencer Leigh

and the hurricane blows through; everything is blown around, it's a cleansing, the whole film is a cleansing.

I need a very firm anchor in that hurricane, the anchor is my inheritance, not my family inheritance, but a cultural one, which locates the film IN HOME.

Would you describe yourself as a patriot?

Yes, I think of Wilfred Owen's parable of the old men and the young saying: 'Abraham slew his son . . . And half the seed of Europe one by one.' The first and second world wars dislocated countries, destroyed Europe; after the last war Europe was occupied.

The Hitlerian soundtrack in the film is about that, particularly in counterpoint to the British Sergeant-Major?

In this the land of Hope and Glory? Who was my father fighting for? Was he fighting a just war? Or any old war? Was it possible to fight for the good cause? Why did they turn the battle against us? Why did they have to introduce the rhetoric of poverty, of virtue through suffering? Very popular in England! Margaret the great flagellator. It's a terrible turning inwards, also a turning away, and a rejection, cold people drowning in wealth; yet in order to retain power they use this rhetoric of povery. Bad news to keep us on edge, to maintain rank. They are the bringers of bad news, the fear merchants.

You're very concerned with origins.

Yes, because I was displaced by sexuality. In some ways we were rootless; remember the faeries? We danced while they put down roots, took out mortgages but the soil was poisoned.

What are you searching for?

The searching is my dynamic. I don't believe in the gold at the end of the rainbow, but I do believe in the rainbow.

And the trip to America?

The pilgrims were after money; puritanism was economic. Fed up with the Catholic Church shilly-shallying about usury, Luther pinned up the bill on the door, the bill that the Catholic Church was going to pay. The money tills chinked in Geneva, it became the banking centre of the world. The banking system in the City of London wasn't working very well in the 1620s so the pilgrims made a break for new pastures and founded Wall Street. After that the rest of us were put up against it. It was all economic, the fathers were just after a quick buck, and, by the way, had great fun killing the American Indians: a happy-go-lucky genocide the sons of England perfected.

They were very good at *lebensraum*, so when you hear Hitler talking about Czechoslovakia on my soundtrack, think of it as a pathetic attempt at the end of history to make a little space. The English were already there: Hitler was an amateur, the British professionals—by the right quick march—and our flag looked better than the swastika, it had more colours in it. I use the Albert memorial, the great masterwork of the 19th century, in the sequence of *Land of Hope and Glory* with the family footage taken by my father when he was seconded to the Pakistan airforce.

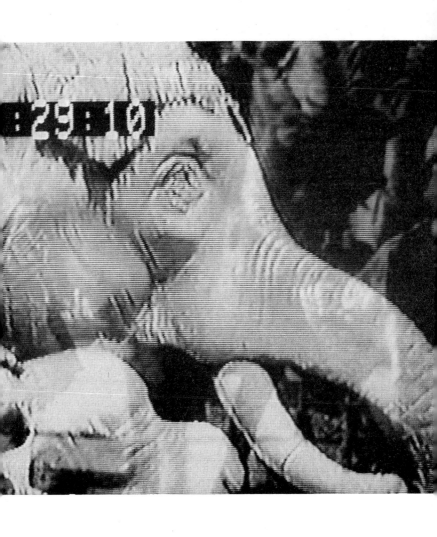

The Last of England: The Albert Memorial

The Last of England: Final Sequence

The Albert memorial, is the summing up, the cross supported by the angels. Prince Albert as paterfamilias in the middle, sitting on art, architecture, music, and the sciences. Spread out at the four corners are the four continents of the earth, of the Empire.

It's the most important 'official' work of the 19th century; it attempts to bring everything together and centralise it under the British Monarchy. The attempt failed.

P.S.

A postcard from Colin McCabe to say that he found it extraordinary how a vision so bleak was at the same time exhilarating, much the same reaction as Tilda on the phone. All the debris of the past thrown out, the cobwebs brushed away, I've done it; now I sit in silence and look at the empty room with the dust floating 'like infinite worlds in a shaft of sunlight'. As I spun round and round on the shingle this afternoon, filming Tilda in the beam of the lighthouse, I thought of Kubla Khan's, 'Weave a circle round him thrice'.

What would the view be from Prospect Cottage? Prospero has returned home, his staff plunged into the roaring nuclear waters, those heavy waters drunk with death, but Miranda stays behind. Here comes the delivery boy on his motorbike with a message 'sign here'. She opens the parcel, as she scrawls her signature. 'What did you say your name was?' 'Ariel.' He has brought a parcel every day this week. I can't tell you what's in them, it's her secret.

V

TEN GO MAD ON THE RIVIERA

The crew of *Aria* met at The Carlton. The dead centre of the Cannes festival, a mammoth *fin-de-siècle* hotel, papered with lurid posters advertising the naked delights of *Sex Sluts in the Slammer*, and *Surf Nazis Must Die*, presided over by the Lares and Penates of the quick buck: Golem and Globus of Cannon films. Razor-sharp smile of cine sharks. Barely up the steps into the crowded hall, we were pushed back, helter-skelter onto the streets to rush to the opening (in the Grand Palais) of Lindsay Anderson's *The Whales of August*, in the presence of their Royal Highnesses.

So muddled is Cannes that at the press-show for the film this morning the paparazzi confused the title of the film with the Princess of Wales, and Lindsay found himself dealing with the gossip columnists of Tout le Beau Monde. Tripping along in our self-conscious glad-rags, ogled by a thousand camera persons, gendarmes, officials and trumpeters. Desperate-looking celebs pushed and jostled us with their gun-toting bodyguards, snarling at by roaring crowds, dresses trampled in a designer death-walk. This way! This way! That way! Selena, Selena, Selena! That way! Carried up the steps in a whirling vortex, to the theme tune of *2001*.

At the other side of the guillotine a miraculous change of perspective. For an hour and a half *The Whales of August* transported us to an old wooden house on the coast of Maine, inhabited by Lillian Gish and Bette Davies. A gossamer film which drew you into a web of love for the two old sisters they played; you wanted to stretch out your hands like Jean Marais in *Orphée* and walk through the silver beam into the magic house. What a contrast to the commercial cattlemarket with its apology of a competition. At one moment Bette Davies, who plays the blind and slightly tyrannical sister, says—'I always had beautiful hair'; time had spared it. Lillian Gish brushed its silver strands, dusted old photos in silver frames, put her own hair up.

When the irascible Bette Davies finally consents to the installation of a picture window: 'We're much too old to do anything new' the radiant surprise on Lillian's face crept upon me so that I nearly fell off my seat. And when she said 'Perhaps we have outlived our time', 'No, No, No,' I could hear the audience shout silently, 'you haven't!'

I've never gone to the cinema to see the stars, but this night I did, and I saw them. Tilda said from the moment the film began you knew you were in good hands. At the end of the film Lillian Gish came onto the stage, far below, a little white butterfly lady from the Kabuki; there she was, we all shouted: 'Bravo! Bravo! Bravo!'

Today the British contingent (contingent is a good word for them) were not so enthusiastic. I kept rather quiet: neither Lindsay nor these two ladies need my help; they are quite canny enough. I, for one, couldn't imagine anyone crossing Bette Davies, who retorted to one critic's praise for Lillian's close-ups: 'Of course she should be good, she invented them with Mr Griffiths in 1916.'

The evening ended at a ponderous dinner for Alec Guiness in the presence of the Prince and Princess of Wales. An orchestra played forgettable tunes from British films, including a number with a boy soprano, which gave the event a musty church-like air.

★ ★ ★

7 out of 10 go mad on the Riviera 1987

Which of the deadly sins threw the bottle to christen *Aria*? What constellations collided to bring us together, to board this ship of fools? To cross unchartered waters? There's Admiral Ken who, you remember, made *Revenge of the Killer Sequins*, and Captain Bob, top of the pops, Altman, bad taste never looked so good, one two, one two, take your partners for the last waltz, it's Billy Bryden, entertainments officer, with Sir John and Lady Hurt dancing, Champagne! Champagne! The end of this journey is dinner our destination *petits fours*.

At 4 am the champagne turns flat in the blood. Jean Paul Gaultier, a truant schoolboy, dances in his shorts under the pines, while Donna Hurt creeps up on her husband, who is being devoured by a Japanese refugee from *Petrouchka*; backless, sideless and damn near frontless she floors him with a flashbulb straight between the eyes, dazed. There's a new type of sequin that blinds you—looks like a permanent star filter—which migrates in the dark, weaving in streams between the aisles. The lights come up to reveal an audience of skeletons: 'Ah the curse of the Killer Sequins', Well done Ken. We've passed by the isles of intelligence and integrity. Is this a movie? Is this a deal? Is this a poster?

DON'T PLAY WITH FIRE

In the newspapers today I read that a fire had been started by a dog chewing a box of matches. 'Don't play with matches. Don't play with fire.' Some of the first words a child hears. Of course, we all played with fire: secretly knowing if we were caught we would bring the house down on ourselves. The picnics in the pine woods of Ostia revolved around the building of a fire. Tinder, matches, fir cones were soon found, and the most delicious sausages were cooked. In the Nissen hut at Cambridge the old coke stoves glowed and emitted sulphurous, choking gases; cleaning out the clinker early in the morning you held your breath. In the '50s the warm hearth scene of childhood reveries was replaced by the cold dictatorial cathode ray. The room no longer faced the fire. The fire became illegal, the choking smogs that hung in London rooms, circling the weak light bulbs, were ordered out. Those dark, mysterious smogs in which the phantoms stalked.

The fire no longer sent messages to Father Christmas, charcoal-black, floating up the chimney. It turned nasty and blazed through the Dorset heath, rhododendrons withered in its path, perhaps some boy burning patterns across an old exam with a magnifying glass.

Fire consumed homes. Butler's Wharf was extinguished, one August night in 1979—what a sense of relief. Fire consumed and cleansed, gave power to the imagination, ordeal by fire. I moved to Phoenix House, out of the ashes. Crematoria are such cold places; who lights the sacred fires?

Fire runs in rivulets through my dreams, consumes everything in its path. In *In The Shadow Of The Sun*, it's

The Last of England: The heretic

organised in a geometric fire-maze, the roses burn. The same maze recurs in *Jubilee*, we are literally playing in fire. Fire informs *The Last Of England*, burning, burning, burning. Can there be too much fire? It flickers across *Imagining October*, sacred fires of Zoroaster. Fire destroys the old, creates a place for the new. Firefly, scintilla, spark, pyromaniac. Turner's 'Burning of the Houses of Parliament', sheets of fire reflected in the waters, rivers of fire, the burning heart of the matter.

VIRUS

You were talking about why you don't miss being promiscuous.

I wasn't, you were telling me why I shouldn't miss being promiscuous. How do you conduct your life, when you might only have the antibodies to the virus, so you could be living your life under an illusion? It leads to a conflict: you may be altering your life for an illusion.

That's the state of medical science.

But it doesn't alter the fact one can't find out. Do you terminate your sexual life, or not? Being middle-aged it's not such a problem, but it is a problem for a young man of twenty-three, much more of a problem. You could refer him to a monastery, but that was free choice; there is no freedom in this. Is it possible to lead a celibate life? That was difficult even for those who had chosen it.

It's hard for intelligent people to accept virtue imposed by fear.

Yes, but it isn't just fear for yourself, it's the fear of hurting someone. It took me a few weeks to come to accept I was body positive; at first I thought this is not true. Then I realised the enormity of it, it had pushed me into yet another corner, this time for keeps. It quickly became a way of life: YOU AND ME, ME AND YOU. When the sun shone it became unbearable, and I didn't say anything, I had decided to be stoic, one of the fathers. This was the chance to be a grown-up. What I really felt was we should all cry, but of course I didn't, couldn't. I walked down the street in the sunlight, and everyone was so blissfully unaware. The sun is still shining.

HOPE

'The little white lies carried her off beyond the cabbage patch.'
'They've murdered her?'
'Yes.'

The virus saps
Yesterday, Today and Tomorrow?
It crosses out
Cancels

Phoenix House 1987

The Last of England: Royal Wreath

You feel apart, so far apart
The others are playing elections
Composing the tunes
Are they yours any longer?
You watch the argument
From a distance
So near but yet so far
Shall I? becomes
Why bother?
Ten foot under
Am I still part of this?
Withdrawal symptoms
Cold cold turkey
I'll strike out
This way
That way
The exits are all wide open
The entrances barred
The virus attacks creation
Creativity withers
The armadillos are tracking you
Tracking you slowly
Down the Charing Cross Road
Are you the swallow who flew
Through the mead hall?
The plane skims through vast
Canyons of Cumulo Nimbus etched
Against blue skies in the setting
Sun Valley after valley
Reveals itself, I've never seen
Anything quite like this
In all my flying time
The jet turns, and the world

Tips up at a crazy angle
Will London fall off?
Slip into the clouds?
We've landed safely
If only the jet had crashed
I gave Mark his door keys
Last Friday he flew to Paris
And never returned, somewhere
In a wood my door keys
Are slowly interred by twelve Autumns
Not marble, nor the monuments
The film is fading now
The burnt Summer blooms pink
How can I explain this?
Lingering
Malingering
I've not written the will
Not acted sensibly
This is hardly sensible
Non sense
I pull myself together
You can't say there's a dull moment
Moment
But the days
The month, the years
What time for what?
Hours, minutes, seconds
I wrestled with the
Angel all night
He returns to haunt me
Last night
I fucked with the angel
Now he is a handful of feathers

The Last of England

I could fill in the forms
My tax returns
My social security, your insurance
Will I stagger into retirement?
Pop off?
Shall I share the food on the fork?
Give you the other cheek?
Turn a blind eye?
My heart was blind
But never my eyes
That would be impossible
Stare into the mirror
You're looking so well Derek
Terribly well
Mark's photos take years away
They say the dead look calm
I've listened to it
The gurgling and rumblings
As the system disintegrates
Turns in on itself
Digests itself
When did you live?
In Borrowed Time
I'll leave the 21st for you
Think of me on New Years Eve
Then
Horro vacui
I might be cured
    By prayer?
    By drugs?
    By a miracle?
Help. And this could
Go on for Months?
    Years?

God help your indecision
I'll settle to ache into
The future
I'll make another film
This time I'll have no subject
There is nothing that consumes me
Only the slow fucking
Of the virus
With love from me to it
I'LL DO IT IN.

AND THE SHIP SAILED ON

Adam and Eve (that's you),
And Pinch-Me-Not (that's us),
Went down to the sea to bathe,
Adam and Eve were drowned,
Who do you think was saved?
PINCH-ME-NOT.

What was Pinch-Me-Not up to? Well, years ago he
danced to a wind-up gramophone on the deck of HMS
Invincible with his mates. Afterwards the lads went below
decks, stripped off, and fucked so hard they forgot the war.
The ship sailed on and on, and reached a desert island. Was
it the Isle of the Dead? I'm not certain. It could have been
Easter Island with its giant statues, or Stromboli, where

in the sulphurous smoke of the volcano, he discovered a wild flower growing 'essence'. He picked it, and pressed it, and sent it home, to the neat little back-to-backs which he had left far behind. His mates were pirates now, deserters, they fucked each other all night; no one came less than eight times; in the dawn they were like a clean room, minds opened. The fucking burnt away the cobwebs, and broke their manacles.

One day, as the sun came up, they reached the very edge of the horizon. They lay in the dawn, crushed in each other's arms, satiated, but still erect. Who made love to whom that night? All the ghosts came to that party: Alexander the Great threw himself to the battalions that died for him, Socrates pronounced a blessing. Many were there secretly, but I'll not give them away. There was Richard Coeur de Lion with Lord Kitchener, who pointed at us and said 'Your country needs YOU'; Gaveston had his cock up Edward's arse; they had minstrels—Tchaikovsky was blowing Britten—and painters to record them: Michaelangelo, Leonardo, Caravaggio. The guest-list was endless and they built their own world far away from yours, with doctors and dentists, bricklayers and ploughmen. The authorities never caught up with them because they were wizards and witches and faeries. It was a queer old world; you can stamp on a fairy ring, but it will bring you terrible luck, and neither you, or your children, who know how sweet the faeries are, will sleep soundly ever again.

THE SOUND OF BREAKING GLASS

My world is in fragments, smashed in pieces so fine I doubt I will ever re-assemble them. The God that rules over the debris is SILENCE: you'll hear him in the wind that chases through the ruins. In the silence I'm impelled to speak, to remind myself of my existence, violating the God.

Do you know what I mean?

My father hated me punctuating my conversation with those words, do you know what I mean?

Other words like 'pardon' were banned, heaven only knows why; I was belted for that one.

Family rituals.

'Do you know what I mean?'

So I scrabble in the rubbish, an archeologist who stumbles across a buried film. An archeologist who projects his private world along a beam of light into the arena, till all goes dark at the end of the performance, and we go home. Home is where one should be, as Dorothy said, clicking her ruby slippers, there's no place like it. Now, I'm not going to duck it, ART is the key. Those who don't know it simply don't live, they exist. It, of course, is an approach to existence, an inner approach to the outer world; it's not just words and music, but gardens, sweeping, the washing-up; it needs no money this archeology of soul, tho' the powers grab it and run it through the projector to blind you. An artist is engaged in a dig. Deep down, depth, 'the way up is the way down', so it's not about bettering yourself or greening suburbia, you're more likely to meet it in the Police Constable's Cesspit.

I find those who have not visited the cesspit have the stink of virtue. Now you project your private world into the public arena, and produce the flashpoint; the attrition between the private and public world is the tradition you discover. All you can do is point the direction that everyone in the audience who wishes to 'travel' has to take. So as you melt into the dark, think of 'silence'. When everyone has taken the path we are all art and no audience.

SPRING

This year the blossoms came out helter-skelter. Spring has been lost in the rush of Summer. Jon Savage called this evening, and we drove to Maryon Park where Antonioni filmed *Blow Up* back in '66. We walked through its deserted and secret glades half-suspecting to find the body beneath a May tree. As we wandered our footsteps fell into the rhythm of the put put of two boys playing tennis. The park meanders across ridges, with distant views of the City. The silence is broken only by the trains which run through a cutting at its southern edge. The park is a blaze of colour, the tulips form perfect pink and red batallions, inclining slightly to the setting sun. Both of us feel this park has a special intimacy, it's so silent. Years ago I queued with my friends to extra in the film, and Ron, my first love, appears subliminally dancing to the Yardbirds in the nightclub sequence.

In the wooded parts of the park the bluebells are out. I remind myself to telephone Tilda to go to Kent and film them. Last year I missed them; it was too dark when we took a side road near Ashford, and drove through a scented wood violet in the dusk. Next morning when I phoned her, she said there were bluebell woods around her school in Sevenoaks. This journey back, on my way to Dancing Ledge last year, we pulled off the main road on a sudden whim to see Canford. Nothing had changed, the school was deserted, the boys were in class. We had hardly stepped from the car before a puffed-up little man confronted us. 'Name' he barked. I was so taken aback by the familiar school-master's tone that I stared at him blankly. 'Name' he repeated. I should have said 'forgotten', but instead said 'I once lived in this building, I just came back to see it.'

'Have you got permission?' he said. Horrible memories of the prison camp.

'Let's get out of here,' I said. He stood with slit-eyed malevolence, puffing his pipe as we left. Tilda's school was surrounded by bluebell woods, but they'd shrunk to domestic patches between well-heeled gardens. There was no place to film, so we took off south, zig-zagging across the border between Kent and Sussex, the sanitised playground of the spiv culture, heavy with big bang ornamental cherries, clotted gateaux pink, smothering the countryside. Past Battle we discovered a triangle of blue-bells at a field's edge, and further on a recently coppiced wood, carpeted blue.

The camera can't record the delicate scent that is the most pervasive quality of a bluebell wood, and through the lens the flowers evaporate in the searing green of the new foliage. We filmed for twenty minutes in slow motion with the camera buried in the flowers. You can't pick blue-bells: they wilt, even as you touch them. How often that happened as a child: the terrible guilt you felt, putting them in water you knew would never revive them. The

Tilda Swinton, New York 1986

feeling of loss the next morning as you threw them into the dustbin. It's easy to murder a bluebell wood.

THE VILLA CHERNOBYL

Last year Julian Cole asked me to play Pasolini in his graduate film *Ostia*. Getting murdered and buried in freezing mud at 4 am as an uncertain sun came up was gruelling, but there was compensation in a trip to Camber Sands where we filmed a desert sequence in the dunes. I took my Super 8 with me and one shot from that day, my shadow racing across the sand, ended up in *The Last Of England*. On the horizon we could see the nuclear power station at Dungeness, marked by a thin plume of black smoke. Was that sunlight contaminated? At that moment in Chernobyl the doom-watch ticked. A week before Tilda and I had walked in the teeming rain in Glasgow; radioactive rain, we joked, and of course it was. Driving back home from Camber Sands I dreamt up a little lead-lined house, 'The Villa Chernobyl', a Geiger-counter ticking in the hall where the grandfather clock used to chime away the hours. A villa remote in time and place, visited by foolhardy adventurers who braved the desert landscape for tea and scones.

The next week I drove to Somerset with Gerard to film on the beach at Kilve, where I spent afternoons as a child constructing driftwood sculptures for the incoming tide to sweep away. At Hinkley Point we took off the road to the nuclear power station which my Aunt Isobel and the village had fought from her cottage 'Great Beats'. Coming over the hill, it looked old and rusty: these power stations generate a strange atmosphere: the slight hum and the occasional whistle deepens the sense that those who ran them have left long ago. You never see anyone behind the walls; perhaps the computers took over and ordered them out.

A week passed and I drove back to Dungeness out of curiosity, and started filming what was to become *The Last Of England*. On all these journeys last Summer I dreamt of a house in the country, as my little room at Phoenix House was bursting at the seams. Even to find a notebook had become a major operation; Andy's furniture was heavy and difficult to move. My room had imposed isolation on me and had somehow outlived its purpose. It was impossible for me to live with anyone—there was nowhere they could put a toothbrush, even the cupboard with my clothes was jammed with paintings. I sensed Tilda was a little disappointed by the bluebells, so I said: 'Don't worry we'll end up at Dungeness which, I promise, is strange and magical.'

First, though, we had to pass Rye, a little Humpty Dumpty picture-postcard town snug on its hill, glimpsed over a sea of rape (is it mere coincidence that this is the most conspicuous crop of post-modern agriculture?) which sends the bees dizzy and clouds the honey. Rye disappears then, and you enter the flatland of the marshes.

Years ago, on the downs of Ashden, I would sit and watch Dungeness B on the horizon, brooding under storm clouds, patches of sunlight blowing in from the west, but never ventured further than the old military canal lined with ancient hornbeam at the bottom of the hill. At night

Gerard surveys his work

the shoreline twinkled with the lights of Greatstone and the marsh disappeared in the dark. Even in the sunlight today it has a secrecy about it. The wind whips the flooded gravel pits, mottling the slate grey water with white sea-horses, and the wire fences of the Ministry of Defence with the occasional red flag waving make you feel an intruder. Dungeness juts into the sea, like the ivory fang of a pre-historic shark. We passed the church at Lydd and turned towards the power station with its avenue of pylons.

Tilda said, 'The landscape is in crisis.' The tawdry houses that stretch along the shingle at Greatstone, now we're close to them, have a terrible impermanence; the great shark-tooth dragon could wake at any moment and brush them into the sea, lapping up the inhabitants with her flick-ering, sticky tongue, brown as old flypaper. If anyone escaped her nuclear breath she would do for them. You can see it on a risqué postcard: mum in her florals, and dad, toothbrush-moustached in his rolled-up trousers, dis-appearing with some good time girls in polka-dot bikinis down that awful maw.

Rivulets of cherry blossom petals blow in sinuous trails across the road. Perhaps they throw confetti at funerals here. At the end of the road you take the turning to the Britannia, a wartime barracks painted goose-turd green, a colour invented by my art master, Robin Noscoe, and perfected by Messers Brodie and Middleton in tins under the pseudonym 'Brunswick Green' (now unobtainable).

When I was 18 I scooped it out and slashed orange through it in a series of megalithic landscapes, painted in the attic of my good friend Güta Minton. The Britannia is next to the old lighthouse at the end of the miniature Romney, Hythe and Dymchurch railway. It's in the Good Pub Guide and, if looks count, it's a winner. Its fortified appearance reflects the Great British drinking habits, fringed with so many archaic laws. Time gentlemen please. From it the blind drunks who stumble out late at night might think they were in the badlands of Montana, a piece of polythene blowing in the dark like tumbleweed across the prairie.

Over there under the walls of the power station is 'Westward Ho', a sad little railway carriage, its back broken by the terrible winter. Last Summer it was For Sale; if someone had bought it perhaps it would have survived the terrible Easterly which froze the pots on my balcony, killing the spring bulbs.

Between the tumbledown shacks succulent seakale sprouts like wreaths from the stones; broom blown flat by the wind hugs the ground. Not much grows in this stony ground and what does is blown into sinister druidical shapes like the ancient holly woods, watered by the salt spray that the wind whips from the waves. We inspected the ruined shacks with their tightly drawn curtains; there are many more of them for sale this year, their occupants have abandoned them to the wind, uneasy. The estate agent's Xerox calls them 'cottages': perhaps shanties would be more appropriate, or hovels.

I take the camera out on the shingle and Tilda runs round in a circle following the beam of the lighthouse which turns without ceasing. We knock at the door of Prospect Cottage, a tiny wooden fisherman's house displaying a 'For Sale' notice, which tosses and turns in the gale. The view is shingle and sea, no fence or garden to cut it off. From the back a wide empty expanse of scrubland with the nuclear power station.

On the way home Tilda said, 'You have to buy it, Derek.' What else could I do? Probate was cleared on my father's estate; both my sister and I had received an unexpectedly large sum of money with some apprehension. Perhaps this final gesture would sink us, disrupt our lives; we called it 'the loot'. Prospect Cottage was near enough to London and would give me the space to end the lonely life that Phoenix House had imposed. I would no longer have to prepare the films there or paint and write on one small desk. Dungeness was so silent. Only the sound of the wind. 'Does the wind ever stop?' I asked the sweet lady who owned the house. 'Sometimes,' she replied. Before we left I thought of Matthew Arnold's *Dover Beach*, the lines kept recurring: 'Down the vast drear and naked shingles of the world.'

'Come to the window, sweet is the night air'

And then I remembered it . . . ?

The sea is calm tonight,
The tide is full,
The moon lies fair upon the straits;
The cliffs of England stand,
Glimmering and vast, . . . glimmering and vast!
Come to my window, sweet is the night air!
Listen! you hear the grating roar of pebbles which the waves draw back and fling
At their return up the high strand,
Begin and cease and then again begin,
With tremulous cadence slow and bring
The eternal note of sadness in.
Sophocles long ago,
Heard it, and it bought into his mind the turbid ebb and flow of human misery.
Now I only hear
Its melancholy, long, withdrawing roar,

Retreating to the breath
Of the night wind down the vast edges drear and naked
shingles of the world.

THE I OF THE STORM

When Tilda dances at the end of *The Last Of England* she
moves into the eye of a storm. I can feel the audience flat-
tened against their seats; if someone dropped a sweet wrap-
per it would take off and swirl round the room; something
vast is conjured, which buffets you so remorselessly, even
memories of the preceding hour are blown from your
mind. As you are hurled into the vortex you expect Mr
Turner to loom out of the mists lashed to the mast, paint-
brush in hand.

Ford Madox Brown: 'Mr Turner, I presume?'

Those neat emigrés setting off for a new life in the new
world would be buffetted by storms like this before they
rebuilt their homes in Canterbury. Perhaps as they sailed
down the estuary they heard the heron's mournful call.
Perhaps they felt they were crossing the Styx, like these
shades, sailing past the sunset into the night.

Chook Chack Chack

Three rising notes in the silence, and the film goes dark.
The names of my friends float by, the projector is off, what
a relief, what did you see? What did I see?

The Last of England: Tilda dances

Was it about anything?
            nothing
            something
I'm not sure, why don't you tell me?
But if you ask me was it worth it? I'd say yes
Goodnight, Thankyou
For your borrowed time

MESMERISED

You warm my burnt-out heart, blow life into the embers, my shadow's shadow. Could our fingers touch across this page, across the fleeting minutes?

The clock is chiming for my time, 12 o'clock, midnight. The traffic converses in the street below, voices in the background, footsteps across the floor above.

One hot summer's afternoon a boy tapping gold leaf out on a cornice, straddling the scaffolding in baggy, washed, blue overalls, smiles and slips out of them, bronze and gold. Naked, he carries on working. There's music, something slow. I'm sitting down below waiting. He says 'How ya doing?'

'Fine! Fine! It's really hot this afternoon.' He picks up a piece of gold on his brush, and gently blows it. It hovers in the air, he moves back so slightly, and it sticks on his sweaty torso. He bends his face down with a grin, attempting to lick it. 'Hey man, you lick if off.' He slides down the scaffold, his overalls falling to the floor. He kicks them idly. He leans against the fireplace, bracing himself against the dark red marble.

It's hard to fight against passion, for whatever it wants it buys at the expense of soul.

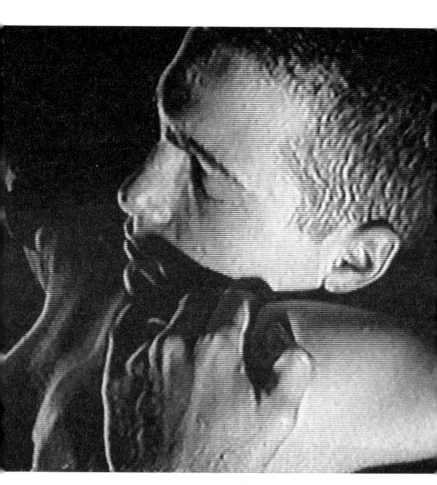

Imagining October